Funny Things That Happen
Humorous True Stories

Once I Had A Crocodile
And Other Tales

A Taxi Through Phnom Penh
And Other Tales

John Aldrick

Refreshingly new and delightful anecdotes from the author's personal experience in Australia and other countries, unique and entertaining, entirely genuine and authentic.

Funny Things That Happen
Humorous true stories

The publishers and author cannot accept responsibility for any errors or omissions, however caused, or for loss or damage occasioned to any person as a result of the material in this publication.

Published in Australia for John M. Aldrick by Angel Key Publications 2020.

ISBN: 978-0-6488738-5-3 Paperback
ISBN: 978-0-6488738-6-0 E-Book

Copyright © John M. Aldrick 2020.

All rights reserved. Without limiting the rights under copyright reserved above, no part of this publication may be reproduced, stored in or introduced into a database and retrieval system or transmitted in any form or by any means (electronic, mechanical, photocopying, recording or otherwise) without the prior written permission of both the owner of the copyright and the publishers.

Published in Australia with the assistance of
ANGEL KEY PUBLICATIONS PTY LTD
https://angelkey.com.au

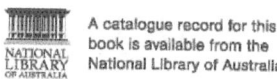

A catalogue record for this book is available from the National Library of Australia

Also by John Aldrick:

Man Versus Mother Earth
   In Loco Parentis

Food, Fatness and Obesity
   The Epidemic of Malnutrition

Fantastic Vegetable Garden Soils
   Grow Your Own!

Field Use Of 4WD Vehicles
   Safe and Certain Outback Travel

Is Recovery From Alcohol Really Worth It?
   One Man's Doubts

Review

John Aldrick acquaints us with these humorous work and life experiences he had whilst travelling through outback Australia and abroad to countries such as Africa, India, the Himalayas, Vietnam, Papua New Guinea, the Philippines and the Indonesian islands to name a few. John's field of work is geomorphology; the study of the land around us, how the earth's surface is formed and changed by rivers, mountains, oceans, air and ice. His role involved a large amount of fieldwork and research, hence the stories. Throughout this book, 'Funny Things That Happen', John's writing style gives you the sense of being there, seeing through his eyes the hands-on and personal experiences dealt with during his travels. Some moments are clearly close to the author's heart. This book is informative for non-travellers who would never experience such occurrences, as these stories include some cultural traditions. There are many laugh-out-loud moments to be enjoyed. Tips on how to light campfires along with the advice for travellers going overseas are a bonus.

M.P. Folkes

About the Author

John Aldrick graduated from Melbourne University with a degree in Agricultural Science and a post-graduate Diploma of Education. He taught in secondary schools, and later gained a master's degree in Tropical Geomorphology from the University of New England. He worked in State and Territory government departments across Australia and in the CSIRO, then as a freelance consultant with international consulting companies around the underdeveloped world as a natural resources specialist.

In the course of his career he worked in every State of Australia except South Australia, a proportion of it involving field work in remote terrain using 4WD vehicles and helicopters, with a team of Australian staff. He also worked in many underdeveloped countries with different nationalities in challenging environments where the normal order of Western countries didn't apply and has had many extraordinary experiences. Some of these events were seriously dangerous, but many were unusual and incredibly funny. A selection of humorous stories from within Australia and in other countries, all of them true, are recorded in this book.

The author spent many years domiciled in Darwin and on the sunshine coast, and lives in his favourite State of Queensland.

Parts I and II

Part I: Once I Had A Crocodile And Other Tales   1
Part II: A Taxi Through Phnom Penh And Other Tales   107

Part I

Once I Had A Crocodile
And Other Tales

John Aldrick

A collection of Australian short stories, incredible and humorous and all true, written in classic Australian outback style.

Author's Note

Australia is a wonderful country. It has the second tallest tree species on earth and the oldest, the second largest but fiercest reptile predator, the most venomous and aggressive snake in the world, a full quota of dangerous spiders, the longest man-made structure ever built, fantastic beaches, magnificent countryside, and our coastal waters are regularly visited by the largest animal ever to have inhabited the earth.

The stories in Part I are set in parts of the Australian landscape where field work or recreational trips in isolated off-road terrain were undertaken. These areas were inaccessible during the northern wet season except by helicopter, but at other times could be reached by competent bushmen with properly equipped 4WD vehicles. The country at the time was in almost pristine condition, a privilege to be in, and it brought out the nature lover in us all. There were often no signs of human habitation, no roads, fences, buildings or people, and self-sufficiency was an absolute necessity.

Apart from small changes to disguise personal identity or provide continuity these stories are all authentic, and actually happened.

Contents

Once I had a crocodile	5
Washing with crocs in the Daly River	9
Crocodile on Lee Point beach	12
Crocodile runs down bullock	15
A German chap with prickly heat	16
Something in the pantry	18
Willie's barramundi	20
A drover feeds his cattle	22
Nearly pissing on the bull	24
Soil survey on Legune	27
Astride the adder	30
One bad morning	32
I hate lawn mowers	35
Invasion by feral pigs	38
Rogue feral buffalo	40
Palmer at Douglas River	44
Annual sorghum – a grass that moves	49
Kangaroo stew or bush turkey?	52
A contrast in fishing techniques	56
Attack by water buffalo	59
A tiny baby bird	61
A frog in a cabbage gum	63
A Northern Territory olive python	65
The boar of Nathan River	68

That bloody spider	71
Anopheles Creek	74
Our camp upon the Ord	78
The cane toad scourge	80
That helicopter pilot	84
Bird eating spiders	86
The ringers' quarters on Mainoru	89
Contretemps with a snake	91
The road to Jim-Jim Falls	93
Bonus: How to light a fire in the bush Even without matches!	97

Once I had a crocodile

My residence in Darwin was never anything like Australia Zoo, but there was a time when my wife wasn't too sure, at least that's the way she phrased it.

Back in those days the Northern Territory was a different place. We didn't have air conditioning or television. Every chance I had I would go out fishing, and I had some quite remarkable experiences, some of them with crocodiles. There were no embargoes, no locked gates, people were honest and straight-forward, there were few tourists, we were all "Territorians", and landholders were always pleased to receive a caller. Visitors to cattle stations in those days would always bring out recent newspapers for the adults and some chewing gum for the kids, and would probably receive some fresh beef or station sausages in return.

I had a mate, a German builder, and he and I and our respective wives drove out one day to visit friends at Munmarlary, a property east of Darwin near the South Alligator River. We each had four-wheel drives and I had a four metre tinny (an aluminium dinghy), and we took along a couple of well packed eskies (ice boxes), one containing food and the other essential drinking supplies. Our welcome having been established at the homestead we drove up the station tracks and fence lines almost to the mouth of the South Alligator River and pitched our camp. The timing was fortuitous, for the river was very tidal there and the tide was coming in, good for catching estuarine barramundi.

We had to wait a little while to go fishing because of the tidal bore, which comes down like a wave at sea and can be quite hazardous, especially if you are near the river bank, where huge chunks of alluvium fall in from the outside parts of the bends with a splash like a breaking wave and a sound like a cannon shot. These tidal bores are normal and occur with most of the higher tides.

We had to be careful in positioning our camp because saltwater crocodiles were abundant in those estuarine parts of the South Alligator, and lots of big ones could be seen on the muddy banks at low tide. These estuarine crocs don't often leave the security of the water, so we could camp fairly close to the river in relative safety, at least for one night. The ones that live for a long time at sea do come ashore at intervals, mainly to stay for a while in freshwater lagoons just behind the coastal dunes to wash out the salt accumulated in their bodies from their sojourn in the sea. During the wet season it's a different story though and large crocodiles will venture overland to find a new lagoon, and they can be dangerous.

In our camp, our wives were busying themselves establishing the cooking arrangements and preparing an evening meal, so we men launched the boat and commenced to fish. We caught some good ones quite quickly – fresh barramundi for dinner!

The evening was very convivial. The really spectacular event was the flight of the flying foxes. We weren't aware of them at first because their home was just far enough away for them not to be heard squabbling during the day, as they constantly do. But just after dusk they launched themselves in a tremendous spectacle, continuously quarrelling, hair and dung raining down, and they flapped off up-river in their droves, using the last of the evening light reflected from the water to guide them. This flying fox colony was so big that those bat-like animals poured out of their tree-top roost and up that river for a solid half an hour. It was already dark enough in the shadows to the sides of the river for them to escape from predators if they had to, because flying foxes are good to eat – so they say. You'd think they ought to be because they're vegetarian, but I found them distinctly oily and somewhat rancid tasting. At that time the Melaleucas were in full flower, not that Melaleuca flowers smell so good I suppose, but that was the food they sought, and that might be why they taste a bit off. Melaleuca does not make good firewood either as it produces very smelly smoke, a bit like the smell of someone pissing on the dying embers of a campfire. Flying foxes cannot take off from the ground because they are heavy flyers and their initial trajectory must be slightly downwards until they pick up speed, so they have to climb up on something to take off, a decent log will do.

The next spectacular event was in the morning, when the tide had settled down a bit and all was smooth and calm. We were out in the tinny once again and no fish were biting, but there were quite a lot of baby crocodiles about. We caught a few just for fun, by sneaking up alongside them in the boat and grabbing them just behind the head. My mate was too slow, he caught one too far down its body and it swung around and bit him on his thumb. I was used to people swearing, but I'd never heard German quite like that before. It soon became time for us to go, and as a souvenir I kept one little croc and took it back to Darwin with me. I don't remember how I carried it, I might have wrapped it in a wet towel but most likely I put it in one of the then empty eskies in some of its own river water, with a rock in there to help the little fellow keep on top and breathe.

Back at home in Darwin as I unloaded the vehicle I thought – what would I do with it now? A crocodile, in suburbia? The absurdity of my rather radical pet keeping proposition was growing on me by the minute, and I resolved to take it down to Rapid Creek and let it go – tomorrow. That was my big mistake, I should have done it immediately. I paused for time and had a tinnie (the beer sort) as one does when faced with a conundrum. Then to the consternation of my wife I placed the thing in a few inches of water in the bath, whilst further lubricated cogitation could be indulged in.

I reasoned that I had responsibility for it now, so at least I ought to feed it. We had some mince, so with a pencil to entice it I made a pass or two before its face (read snout) and suddenly it got the message, and chomp! It grabbed the pencil in its mouth, and did it bite! I felt afresh for my German mate. I got the pencil back later, but its tiny teeth were very sharp and almost cut the pencil in two. With some trepidation, I pushed a small amount of mince down its throat and left it in the bath until tomorrow, and put it out of my mind.

A short time later there was a desperate hullabaloo. Now you need to know that at that time my wife was a feline aficionado, and she also had an invited friend from the south staying there with us. Coming from the general area of the bath was a gross thrashing about in the water, sounds of real panic, accompanied by loud distraught meows from one of the establishment's cats. I don't know who won the sprint to the bathroom, but it was probably my wife, cursing all reptiles in general and my pet one in particular, whilst trying to rescue and placate her cat. The damn thing was in there with my crocodile!

I'm not sure who was the most afraid, the cat, the croc, my wife or me. My wife's friend from the south kept well away, she was still recovering from the green frogs in the toilet, not to mention the cane toads infatuated by the back door light because it attracted heaps of insects, and a crocodile cavorting with a cat in the bath-tub seemed to be just a little too much for her at the time. I guess the cat had wondered what was in the bath, curious as cats are, and had slipped and fallen in. I don't know all the facts but reconstructing from the sounds, I took it that both cat and croc had frightened each other senseless, and completely inconsiderate of each other and without a thought for proper protocol had ricocheted around the bath, not even pausing in their haste to pass the time of day. By the time order was restored both animals had defecated liberally, and a spray of malodorous water covered half the room.

It took a while to live that one down!

Washing with crocs in the Daly River

It is quite a skill, bathing with crocodiles, dangerous too, but sometimes it has to be done. We had it down to a fine art.

We were working in the bush in the Fish River area on the western side of the Daly River, Northern Territory. We knew of a secluded place on the river south of the Daly River settlement and just upstream of the tidal limit, quite isolated, with a beautiful beach and tall shady frontage vegetation. The river here was wide and mostly deep, but there was a rocky bar there that had been a crossing place many years ago. The old crossing was washed away now but it was still possible to drive across the river if you knew how to do it and selected your path carefully. We had several times gone to this spot for water. We used to back our vehicles into the river and bucket water into the on-board tanks, using a chain of three men.

On this particular occasion, we came out of the bush where we were working at the end of a very hot day, our work completed, feeling sweaty and dirty, and decided to drive the twenty or so kilometres to the Daly as a treat so that we could camp in that nice spot, fill our water tanks and have a decent bath. It was near the end of the dry season and things were tough in the bush. Mobs of Agile Wallabies were sheltering under all the trees that offered any shade at all. The ground below these trees was completely covered with wallabies, and as the sun moved westerly they would move around with the shade, sometimes digging up and eating the hairy roots of a wiry grass, Chrysopogon fallax, because there was nothing else.

Our camping place was a bit back from the river where the danger from crocodiles was not so great. There, we could enjoy the sounds of the river, the calm, reassuring flowing and babbling of the water over the bar, and the coolness of the large shady paperbarks, Leichhardt pines, banyans, pandanus clumps, ghost gums, and the multitude of vines and creepers and other lush vegetation along the river bank. And we could easily walk from there to that beach beside the river for a bath. What a change from where we'd been!

But the river here was full of crocodiles. At night by torchlight there were many red eyes along the far bank and upstream and downstream from us, watching. It was definitely unsafe to bathe here. Many of these crocs were of the freshwater variety and lived on fish, not so much on land animals. But saltwater crocs were there as well, and although they were probably somewhat naive, we had filled our water tanks and camped here a few times before and they would have recognized us, for saltwater crocodiles are quick learners, especially where food is concerned, and they do remember things. I wouldn't try what we were going to do now with anybody other than my staff, who were quite experienced with crocodiles.

It was getting dark by now, but we were very grimy and had to have a bath, so we executed our tried and proven strategy. We went down to the river together. We all stripped off except one man, he held my rifle, a heavy-duty centre-fire one, loaded and ready just in case, and a powerful torch. He played his torch up and down the river, watching for movement among the red eyes (the green eyes are buffalo). We placed another torch on the sand, illuminating the spot on the beach where we were standing. Naked, we each took up our cake of soap, and on the word "go!" we rushed into the river and wet ourselves all over, crocs or not, then rushed back out again onto the beach. On the beach, we soaped and washed ourselves all over, taking care not to drop our soap because sand sticks to it, and stays there for the life of the cake. Then, again on the word "go!" we rushed back into the river and rinsed the soap off as fast as we could, with much splashing and shouting, really enjoying getting ourselves cleaned off and cool. Then we were out again, and back up the beach to where we had left our clothes. All that took only a short time actually in the water, not enough for the crocodiles to react. But we didn't get dressed just yet, there was still one of us to go.

One "clean" man then took over the rifle and another one the torch, and our watchman on the bank stripped off and repeated our performance. He did the same thing we had done but on his own, whilst we kept watch over him. His bath was riskier than ours because by now the crocodiles were alerted, roused and watching, and more inclined to move in for a kill.

We were in the water for less than a minute overall, but that was long enough, we had enjoyed a great bath and left the beach feeling quite refreshed, and it was all too fast for the crocs to get their act together and sneak up with any ill intent. Back at camp we boiled the billy, cooked a meal, had a yarn, and satisfied, we went to bed inside our swags and slept a peaceful sleep.

Next morning, we fitted a snorkel to one of the vehicles, slackened off the fan belts on all of them, and with a vehicle close behind for safety, one man waded out to find a place to cross. The crossing place changes its character every year after the wet season floods. The main problems were large boulders and deep holes in the riverbed which change position from year to year. The water depth was over the bonnet in places but the flow was not very strong, and these vehicles were all diesels, and we got all three of them over with no problems, re-instated the fan belts, dried out our brakes and headed off to Tipperary Station.

We all felt good, but what a way to have a bath!

Crocodile on Lee Point beach

I've had a bit to do with crocodiles, most of it incidental, and generally they put the wind up me to a degree. But there was one, close to Darwin, that frightened the proverbial out of me.

When I first lived in Darwin back in the 1970s and 80s I was a runner. I loved to run, and most mornings at about dawn saw me on the roads or some lonely beach doing my several kilometre run. I liked the beaches best, particularly the more distant pristine ones such as Lee Point beach. Most people preferred Casuarina beach because it was closer to town and had better access; the two actually converged at Lee Point. There was only a nominal road to Lee Point in those days, and access from there to the beach and the dunes behind it was by four-wheel drive vehicle only. Darwin people did go to Lee Point, but mostly later in the day or towards sunset in the afternoon, particularly on weekends. So in the early mornings around sunrise I invariably had that beach to myself.

The beach was best at low tide because there was a huge expanse of sand exposed that I could run on. It was not uncommon for me to find the tracks of a turtle that had come ashore to lay her eggs, or sometimes the turtle herself. Crocodiles were there as well, and I had heard the odd one barking amongst the mangroves. Some of these were big crocs and I was suitably impressed, and careful to keep out of their way. There was also a small fresh-water creek that followed along behind the fore-dune and fed into a tidal inlet towards the eastern end of the beach, and although I had never seen one, I knew that saltwater crocodiles would be there in that creek from time to time.

On this particular morning the beach was quite charming, beautiful in the early morning light, each ripple in the sand casting a long thin shadow, the footprints of migratory birds, and little fish and crabs marooned in pools of sea water left behind by the tide. I was there a little earlier than usual, and as I usually did, I checked for crocodiles before beginning my run. There was nothing, no crocs in sight, only peace and quiet and tranquility, and so I began to run. Off I went, not too fast at first, just jogging along to warm up before I hit my running speed. My thoughts at peace, my mind in neutral, I ran to exercise, treading softly on the sand, running as an automaton, and onwards down the beach I went. The track I chose was a little seaward from the fore dune, just below the high tide mark, because the sand there was firmer and easier to run on.

Then all at once there was a racket, a splashing rustling sound, and a huge, great crocodile erupted, monumental, from the mangrove creek behind the dune. It bolted out towards me, straight towards my track, sand spraying from its wake, with a flush of birds lifting from the trees behind. Now crocs can run, and quickly too, and this was now its prime directive. My eyes on stalks, I saw that croc, it wasn't far away, it seemed clearly to be after me and intent on getting to me in a hurry. Saltwater crocodiles have the most powerful jaws of any animal on earth, much stronger than sharks and 4-5 times stronger than a lion, they have been compared with Tyrannosaurus Rex. A big saltie with its snout wide open is worse than a heavy-duty excavator.

I recalled the adage, to be eaten is not an illustrious end to one's career.

Now I could run, right up with the best, but there could never be a man so quick, no-one could be as fast as I against that beast. I turned around away from it, that crocodile just disappeared from view, and there in front of me were all my outward tracks, which I was now re-consuming at a quite spectacular rate, but with a much-extended stride. I ran, with full revs on my legs, way past where I had parked my vehicle. If I'd had sufficient traction in the sand I might have shot around the point and gone on down Casuarina beach as well. And I tell you what, that crocodile got nowhere near, I ran Olympic best, I didn't look or turn my head or stop until I'd paced out way beyond the gallop of that croc.

And then at last I heard a splash, I looked around, the croc was in the water. He was in the sea, right below the point where he had burst upon the beach. He wasn't chasing me at all, he was quite as scared as I, and was just heading for the water. He was probably quietly cresting the dune from his sojourn in the creek when all at once he was accosted by a man, running straight towards him. He'd panicked, and bolted for his sanctuary, the sea. And there was he, and here was I, both of us extremely frightened and running for our lives, but each in different directions. Though he could bite and would if trapped, that was not his aim, he only sought the water, from creek to sea he went, and I mistook his intent.

Looking back along the beach the flying sand had settled, and I reckoned that I'd had exercise enough, and plenty. As I wandered thankfully back towards my vehicle, I noted that my tracks resembled those of a spirited and somewhat deranged turtle, sculling horizontally along the beach. So did the crocodile's, but at right angles to mine, straight towards the sea. I tell you true, that beach was wild, on that dramatic morning!

Crocodile runs down bullock

I had cause to travel down an old stock route, it was a work venture, and I had planned it thoroughly. I couldn't use a helicopter because it was a very long way and I couldn't have kept fuel up to it, so we were in heavy-duty four-wheel drives. No-one could find that route again, even the locals hadn't heard of it, I found it on old aerial photographs. It suited my purpose very well, if I could follow it. It started south from Borroloola. The first remaining vestiges of it began at Seven Emu Station where the nearby part of it was still being used as a track, and I joined it there. The manager was a part Aboriginal and very reliable, and he told me this story. He saw this with eyes that only an Aborigine can, and I report it faithfully. It had been a heavy wet season and all the land was saturated. He was on horseback, out in a paddock far away from his home. Close before him, a huge crocodile erupted out of silent cover and rushed across the land. They can really run, they get up on their legs and hold their tail up like a monstrous lizard and scutter along at breakneck pace, but for a short distance only, you can't rush a ton of reptile along very far very fast. Then that crocodile selected and ran down a beast. A lizard, capturing a bullock! On dry land! Savaging it! Primal! City people just don't know, nor southerners. What he remembered most was the bellowing of both of them, and the spray of water all around. He didn't want to be out in the paddock with that kind of stuff going on, and his horse wasn't going to either.

He said (and this might not be true) that he beat his horse back to the homestead!

A German chap with prickly heat

Australian bushmen have some amazing cures for ailments of all kinds, and I've been privileged to see some of them in operation. Without a doubt, the cure for prickly heat I saw applied on this occasion was one of the most spectacular.

I was friends with the German community in Darwin and used to go out bush with some of them, fishing, swimming, and generally enjoying the bush. The best time was just after the wet season had ended, usually in April at about Easter time. At that time the creeks and waterfalls were still running strongly, the grass was green and high, everything was clean and washed and pristine, and access to the best spots was just becoming possible. It was strictly four-wheel drive access though because there were still wet patches, washouts, and water crossings to ford, which meant that very few if any people were out and about and we had the bush virtually to ourselves.

One of our favourite spots was UDP Waterfall on the edge of the Arnhem Land escarpment, named after an old mine nearby, and at this time of year the fall was still running heavily and it and the pool below it were quite full, crystal clear and beautiful, very pleasant indeed. The pool was lined with huge paperbark trees and pandanus palms, and spray from the waterfall wafted half across it. Another spot not far distant was Koolpin Falls, a series of large deep pools each with its own waterfall. The creeks in all these places were full of black bream, easy to catch and delicious on fresh buttered bread. There were many birds about, file snakes in the lagoons, multicoloured frogs, spritely little green spiders with bulbous eyes hopping around in the grass, and dragonflies were everywhere.

On this occasion I was camped at UDP Falls with some of my mates and a couple of Germans new to Australia who hadn't been out bush before. They loved it, and we all swam and fished and basked in the brilliant warm sunshine, with the odd beer to bridge the halting English the new chaps had. It was very humid, and a swim every now and then was almost mandatory. The new arrivals were not used to the heat and humidity, and one of them in particular developed prickly heat – a red and pimply rash that becomes very itchy and irritable. He had it over much of his body, in his armpits, all around his groin and bottom, inside his elbows and on his chest, and much advice was bandied around on how to cure it.

The cure this chap liked the sound of best was the methylated spirits cure. "Metho" rubbed into the affected areas was said by most to be a sure-fire cure. So he thought he would do a trial of it, starting with his chest. Now he had a large and hairy chest and it took quite a lot of metho to cover it in any decent concentration. But he did it, then carefully closed the metho bottle and put it well away. Then he took out a cigarette and struck a match to light it. There was a "whoosh", a shimmering electric blue flame, and his hairy chest was well alight. The next "whoosh" was him diving into the pool, with even the hair on his head on fire.

He came out from the pool with a bare chest, no eyebrows, frizzy hair, and a wondrous sort of look, as if to say that sure, his prickly heat had gone, but he thought that the Australian types of cure were just a little drastic. In a loud but querulous voice accompanied by some interesting gestures he informed us of this opinion, and his final words on the matter were to the effect that he was pleased that he only did a trial, and didn't apply the metho to all his other itchy parts as well!

Something in the pantry

It must have been after midnight when I awoke. I could have sworn that it was a strange noise that had awakened me; was there something peculiar in the house? I lay there half holding my breath – yes, there it was again! It must be in the kitchen, I could hear jars and packets being moved. But the dog wasn't barking, so it couldn't be an intruder. A poltergeist? The sound again, no mistake, something was in the house! A rat? A snake? We get some pretty big pythons here, it could have come in through the cat door. A venomous one?

I crept out of bed, grabbed a broom and slid down to the kitchen, my wife following some way behind. The noise again! I had nothing on and was feeling vulnerable, as men do when naked. I carefully entered the kitchen, searching for the culprit. But no, there was not a thing in evidence. I crept up to the pantry and peeped inside, but there was nothing there that I could see. I turned on the pantry light, but still nothing. The sound had ceased by now, but something was definitely in there somewhere, and strong enough to move substantial things about. I went back to the bedroom for my torch. Then I returned and looked again, peering along the shelves, but still saw nothing.

I eventually turned the pantry light off and stood there, listening, still holding my torch, with my wife looking over my shoulder. And then I saw it; a pair of beady eyes on the bottom pantry shelf, reflecting in the torchlight! Instantly I grabbed my wife and whipped her out of the doorway, the eyes on this thing were far enough apart for it to be a very big snake, if it was one, and I wasn't taking any chances. I looked in carefully again. And as I gazed the eyes took on a shape, and there before me squatted a possum, about half grown. It had come inside to find a spot to stay, and where better than in our pantry, well sheltered and fully found!

By now the dog was interested too and was striving to be involved. I took the broom and tried to evict the possum, but all I succeeded in doing was to chase it around the shelves, upsetting bottles, jars and bags; flour, tea and sugar were going everywhere, until at last I flushed it to the pantry door, and then grab! The dog had it by its back. "Good boy!" I shouted. "Take it out!" And he did. He rushed straight out with it, then there was a strangled yelp. The possum must have turned around and bitten him. Next there was a scuffle, and the possum came back in again at the double, closely pursued by a somewhat chastened and much more careful dog.

Well, what followed was vaudeville. I chased that possum around the kitchen, through the lounge, over the furniture, and the dog chased it too, and what a mess we made. Do you know what possums do when cornered? They piss, and possum piss pongs. But the possum was getting the hang of it now and after every few circuits it darted back into the pantry, re-affirming its new ownership rights. My wife had lost her grip by now, and quite starkers, had given way to wild abandoned mirth, intermixed with shrieks as yet another household icon tumbled.

But the dog and I were winning; we eventually had that possum in the passage and were chasing it along towards the bathroom, where we could surely corner it. What a ridiculous sight we must have made, the possum, thoroughly disenchanted by now, lolloping down the passageway, closely followed by the dog, a very cautious dog, his interest now confined to keeping his nose jammed up against the possum's rear orifice, then me with my broom, completely naked, trying to shepherd it, shouting instructions to the world at large, and last of all my wife, running along behind as naked as the day she was born, determined not to miss a thing. What a sight! Thank goodness it was dark, and we had no near neighbours.

In the bathroom I threw a towel over the possum and caught it, and with some difficulty put it out a window, and we never saw it again. I eventually got my wife back to bed and checked her hysterics, and left the clean-up till the morning. But the dog was grinning widely, panting, wanting more, he'd never had so wild an interlude!

Willie's barramundi

It wasn't entirely his fault but as circumstances were a barramundi bit Willie on his dick – tried to make off with it in fact. Ever had a barramundi chewing on your thing? This particular fish did the equivalent of the crocodile death roll, it thrashed about in a frenzy, frightened because there was a man there, but trying to have Willie's willy for lunch anyway. Barramundi have very hard and bony jaws, not at all what a man might be used to. Willie kicked up a tremendous fuss about it, more so than the barramundi did (which I thought might have had a better case), but after all, he owned it, it was his willie, and he was entitled to complain. You could have heard him halfway back to Darwin. That he had been hurt I don't deny, and with an assault like that you couldn't blame him, but I still think that his performance was a bit optional. It happened like this.

We were in the Northern Territory fishing, out on the coastal plains, in the days when crocodiles had been shot at for so long that it was almost safe to swim again. Willie was my friend, a German fellow, and we liked to fish. We both had four-wheel drives and I had a four metre aluminium dinghy. Willie had his girlfriend with him, a beautiful blonde white Russian. We were fishing in a creek which flowed into Yellow Waters lagoon close to Jabiluka, where they now mine uranium. It was very hot indeed and having caught several nice fish we all stripped off our clothes and sank gratefully into the cool waters of the lagoon. All was peace and tranquility.

And then came something utterly beyond my comprehension. For no apparent reason Willie suddenly produced a martial roar, and began to leap about. He was still in the water but was thrashing around, going down and coming up, at intervals appearing even to walk upon the surface, bashing at his body, uttering unintelligible anguished animal sounds, and clearly in urgent and dire distress. This extreme agitation had come upon him suddenly, something was very wrong with Willie. This was unusual, not like him at all, and I began to gather that something was more than a bit astray. I swam to help. Then I think he must have had a realization, or perhaps he formed some sort of opinion, but incredibly he seemed to get even less logical.

Willie was a strong and virile man. With a tremendous spray of foam followed by a cloud of russet dust he leaped out of the water and bolted up the bank, he might even have gone up on all fours, I can't remember. I was flabbergasted, he rushed right up that bank, and in record time he made it to the top. And his companion, the white Russian woman, was with him in sympathy and collusion, in fact I think she might have beaten him to the top. At that time neither she nor I had any idea of what had ailed him, but she must have reckoned that his behaviour seemed to be a fair thing and mimicked his example. I recalled that she was blonde, and thus dismissed her case.

But that was not the end of it, not by far. For quite some time my friend Willie leaped around the bush lamenting, howling, bashing through the scrub, holding his lower body, crying "bloody hell" and uttering other imprecations in what seemed to be various different languages, and his white Russian girlfriend did the same in emulation. I've never heard German like it, or Russian, for that matter. It was really quite spectacular.

Now bear in mind that the fishing was quite good there, in that creek. I didn't know it then but I do now that the cause of Willie's distress was a barramundi, a surface feeder, which had seen a flopping piece of prey and grabbed it, just as though it was a trailed fishing lure. There was no way that this hungry barramundi was going to let that delectable morsel go, be it German, sausage, or whatever. I couldn't understand him at the time because he was somewhat incoherent. To me it seemed quite funny, but Willie was quite substantially upset. So was his girlfriend, though I suspect from a different point of view.

It was only later that I thought, thank God it wasn't me, I couldn't have coped with that blonde!

A drover feeds his cattle

There was a devastating drought upon the land. This was the year 2002, and all the farming and grazing land in country New South Wales was down to bare soil and there was just nothing to feed to stock, it all had to be bought in. Feed was dear, and sometimes it was not to be had except from long distances away, mostly from land that could still be irrigated. Lots of mobs of cattle were on the road, not that there was much left in the "long paddock" either. It was interesting and remarkable to watch the eyes of farmers when a truckload of nice green hay passed through the town of Cowra – I swear that some of them followed those trucks, just to see a bit of green for once and catch a whiff of that smell!

I was parked at the junction of the Reids Flat-Cowra road with the road to Woodstock one afternoon, on my way to Cowra. A truckload of hay, good prime green stuff, coming from the direction of Woodstock had pulled up at the junction, and the driver seemed to be in indecision as to which way to turn. Close behind him was a drover with a mob of travelling cattle, and these cattle were really starved for good green feed; they'd been eating strands of wiry roadside grass and even dried up bits of bark, and hadn't seen a bale of hay for weeks, let alone a green and fragrant one.

The drover was out in front of his mob. The mob behind him began to run, and you can imagine in which direction! Now this drover knew a thing or two, and thought that here was a chance to get a few free mouthfuls of hay for his half-starved stock. He moved his horse right up to the trucky's cab and began to help him with his directions. It's hard to beat a drover; he made sure he blocked the rear-view mirror so that the truckie couldn't see behind him, but he must have wondered why his truck was rocking about a bit.

Now that drover spun it out, he confused the truckie all he could, suggesting one route and then another, all the while blocking the trucky's rearwards view.

Well, at the back of the truck it was pandemonium. Cattle were scrambling for a bite of that hay, ripping and tearing it out from the bottom row of bales, chomping and gulping for all they were worth. The crush was terrific, cattle shoving in, the hungriest ones getting furthest in, and when one of them got his tongue into the hay the others could hardly move him aside. Some even tried to mount the truck, they reared and put their front hooves up onto the tray and started on the second row of bales. It was hunger at its best, and in just those few minutes a very considerable amount of that hay was voraciously consumed.

It had to end, and the truckie decided it was time to go, and he took off to the right, towards Cowra. It took a while, but a couple of gear changes on he did outpace those cattle and continued on his way. It still beats me why he didn't look back in his mirror, perhaps he did, but maybe he had been so confused by the drover that he just headed off without a backward glance. I'd like to have seen his face though, when he arrived in Cowra and saw that quite a chunk of his hay was gone.

I did see the drovers face though, and truly, he was smug, and I swear his cattle looked smug too, as they whiffled at the surface of the road, collecting all the last fallen wisps of hay.

Nearly pissing on the bull

I've always been a bit wary of scrub bulls, especially the old shorthorn types, because they seemed to have a very short fuse and would usually attack if at all provoked. This time I had a lucky escape indeed.

We were mapping land on Bauhinia Downs in the Northern Territory gulf country. Our helicopter work was done, and we were mopping up in four-wheel drives, visiting the last few inspection sites we hadn't been able to land at in the chopper. Timing was important, because the Station had just finished mustering their stock and were about to fly over in their helicopter and shoot all the scrub bulls that remained. These old shorthorn bulls were pretty cunning and some of them wouldn't be mustered from the air, they would just walk under a tree or into the side of a dry creek bed and stay there, no matter how much the pilot tried to shift them with his machine and its hooter. The Station management wanted to put out Brahmans, but all these un-musterable shorthorn bulls had to be disposed of first, by shooting them.

Nearly all the cattle remaining after the muster seemed to be bulls, and most were very aggressive. Scrub bulls in the wild are a serious menace to one's health. They are huge, fierce, carry awe-inspiring horns, run wild and rampant through this country, and can be a real problem. I carry a powerful rifle quite capable of killing a bull, because I had a team of men to protect when we were on the ground walking. I have warned a few of those bulls off in the past with over-the-head shots.

When we sought permission to work on the Station's land, as we always did, we were told sure, go ahead, but not on Friday, because that was the day they were going to do the shooting from their helicopter, and we might accidentally get shot, or chased by one of those irate bulls. So we left it until the following Monday, and then set about our task. To avoid a lot of cross-country scrub-bashing, because the scrub was pretty thick and difficult to traverse, we utilized all the tracks and fence lines that we could to help in getting access to the country.

At the end of one day we had travelled down a long fence line to a dam, and planned to camp there for the night. We were fully mobile; we usually just threw our swags out on the ground or onto a stretcher and cooked a meal and boiled up a brew wherever it was convenient. On this night, we had camped about 50 metres from the fence line, and something similar from the dam. We cooked and ate our meal and went to bed, and slept the sleep of tired men.

It was quite a cold night. I guess there are times in every bushman's life when he dreams up ways of urinating on the ground outside from snug inside his swag, to avoid the hassle and the cold of getting up at night. This is impossible in ordinary circumstances because a man cannot manoeuvre his apparatus adequately to the edge of his stretcher without overbalancing and falling out of bed. All sorts of schemes with tubes and pipes have been devised.

The only system I heard of that seemed at all feasible was trialed by one of my men, but he had a meltdown whilst trying to make it work and all he succeeded in doing was to piss into his swag, and then in mortification, urgently trying to retrieve the situation, he rolled his camp stretcher into the mess as well.

Despite the cold, I wasn't intending to try out the tubes and piping, but tea is known to be a diuretic, and accordingly I awoke at some early morning hour and arose from my swag to relieve myself. Not wanting to foul our campsite I walked off towards the fence for twenty metres or so. It was pretty dark, but there was starlight enough to guide me for that short distance, and I began to piss. I was part-way through when suddenly a most frightening sound erupted; a deep, rumbling, ominous, roaring sound, coming from right in front of me, virtually from the place where I was pissing. Hell! It was one of those scrub bulls!

Picture my plight – half asleep, nothing on, in the middle of a dark night, separated from my swag and vehicle, caught in mid piss, confronted at point blank range by a cranky old scrub bull that had avoided being shot, and there was I, adding insult to injury by pissing virtually on top of him. That bull had come down the fence line in the dead of night to drink at the dam and was confronted by our camp. I guess he stopped and looked at us, smelled our scent, feeling fear and loathing mixed, not knowing whether to proceed and drink or turn around and melt away. He had come in silence, waited, watched, and stood his ground as I approached to piss.

No-one but me will ever know how I felt at that moment, but I can tell you that I came awake very quickly, and as the rumble escalated to a roar I backtracked as fast as I could towards my swag, not that my swag was any place of refuge, I should have gone straight for a vehicle. The others woke at the commotion and quickly took in the situation, but the bull was heading off, crashing through the scrub, and so they all just stayed in bed.

They would not believe that I had almost pissed right on the bull, but they did note that I still hadn't stopped pissing!

Soil survey on Legune

There's nothing like a hard and dirty job out on a shadeless, sunbaked plain to put men into a frame of mind that focuses on cold beer. We were out on Legune Station and running out of water, and after doing minor fence repairs and putting out a small grass fire (as one does, to help) we came across a station bore. We were keen to replenish our water supply, so we pulled up beside a defunct and broken down Southern Cross windmill, checked out the Lister diesel that had replaced it, fuelled it up, cranked it over to start it, filled our water tanks, and put some water into the cattle troughs as well. That was fine, and we went back out onto the plain to continue with our work.

We had been hammering down a hollow soil-coring tube with a Pionjar petrol powered jackhammer to a metre and a half in depth, then pulling it back out again with a special jack, and sliding the soil core out of it for inspection and description. The tube we were using had originally been only a metre long, so back in Darwin an additional half a metre had been welded onto it to give us our required length. But on the next sample the welded joint in the mid part of the tube broke as we tried to jack it out; I guess the weld had been weakened by all the work it had already done. We then had to retrieve the lower part of it from the depths, and that meant digging it out. That was not too bad really because the soil there was sandy and easy to dig, but it still took a quarter of an hour of digging to get our extraction jack in place on top of the buried section and pull it out. Now we had to mend the tube, but how?

We detoured across to Legune Homestead to make repairs but there was no-one there, so we accepted absentee hospitality as was the custom, and started up the station's welder. But its engine had a broken governor and it was responding wildly to power demand. So, with one man controlling the governor manually I did the welding as best I could. But I couldn't do a proper job, the current was just too variable. However, we did manage to stick the two parts of the tube together, albeit roughly. I couldn't remove the slag from inside the tube, but I thought that the soil coming up through it later on would do that. We left a calling card, but the managers of Legune probably still don't know about this unless they saw some signs of our endeavours, or their Aborigines told them about it.

Then a sequence of events was put in train. We went out onto the plains again, but this time the soil was not sand, it was clay. It was covered in thick residues of grass and prickly shrubs (Acacia bidwillii) and the odd small Whitewood sapling (Attalaya hemiglauca) and even walking was difficult. In places, it was so rough that it would have been easy to twist an ankle, and any step was peril. We hammered that tube down through a metre and a half of thick, black, heavy clay and began to jack it out. And then, that bloody tube, it snapped again, but this time the bottom part of it was more than half a metre underground, and it was down in heavy clay! So much for my welding. In order to get purchase on that bottom piece of tube with our jack to pull it out we had to dig a pit almost a metre deep, in heavy black clay soil, in mid-afternoon, the hottest time of day, in the pre-wet season, when it was as hot as hell and oppressively humid as well, and we had no shade, nothing cold and no other options. It was not like the time before. We didn't say a lot, though I know we thought a fair bit. We all just pitched in there and dug, regardless. We had to. We understood very clearly what was before us, and we went in there and laboured, resigned to it; we really worked that time. All that clay had to be loosened bit by bit with a crowbar; it took us hours.

I won't say much about that afternoon, we sweated there for ages, we had no other coring tube and our only choice was to get that remnant out. So we dug, and dug, and dug in turns, sweltering in that hot and sticky heat under that blazing sun, stripped to our undershorts, grappling with that bloody clay, going down a few centimetres at a time, saying little, mostly functional words, apart from the odd loosened epithet, but meaning many. Eventually, quite close to sundown, we got the damn thing out, packed away our gear, and faced our future.

Now that team of men were in my charge, they were supposed to answer my direction, but the four wheel drive in front of mine where all the digging had been done from just started up its engine, and then the one behind me, both their communicating radios turned off from mine, and with one accord they both pulled out and headed straight for Kununurra. And then without a word from me, my driver quickly followed suit as well, he didn't even ask me.

It didn't take a lot of thought on my part, I knew they'd done their duty for the cause and now required their due, which was going to be some considerable time inside the Kununurra pub, their mouths by now exceedingly dry, and salivating at the prospect of refreshment. It was rebellion, a coup, there'd clearly been collusion, they just took off, without a word from me, or any of my sanction.

Now I may be dumb but I'm not stupid. I've never been a hard man, nor a disciplinarian. And it ought be known that on this occasion I had worked as hard as any of them and had lost my load of sweat as much as them or more, and I knew just how they felt. It was also true that there was no way that I could control them, they were going to Kununurra no matter what; I was going to have no say in it at all. But they may have guessed a thing or two, that there was no way I'd object. I didn't have to tell them, they knew; I'd have gone to Kununurra too, no risk, completely at my choice, I'd even have suggested it, led them, persuaded them in fact, because there was no way I was camping on that bloody black soil plain either.

In the Kununurra pub it took several beers apiece before any words did flow, and the first of those were quite explicit, very clear and focused, distinctly in the vernacular, and a lot less than erudite.

Astride the adder

I didn't know that I could levitate, but there's no other explanation for it. Perhaps it was because all the things that were happening at the time were so strange and out of keeping. This was on the Gulf coast, way up north close to the southern border of Arnhem Land, where we were undertaking a large soil survey job. We arrived there in the helicopter, and had landed in a natural clearing right beside a tidal inlet. It was a remote and peaceful place, no natural sounds to speak of, except for a bird or two, and our own quiet talking and footfalls in the grass. Then the trouble started.

Unbeknownst to us a trawler was there also, anchored in the inlet, almost hidden by the mangroves. When we saw it, my team were keen to go on board and see the boat and its catch and have a chat with the crew, and upon invitation that's exactly what they did. Later, as they left the trawler and were heading back towards our chopper, just by chance a twin-engine coastal surveillance aircraft flew right overhead on a routine patrol of this remote stretch of northern coastline. Well, you can imagine what they thought! A rendezvous between a coastal ship and a helicopter, on one of Australia's most remote stretches of coastline! Men walking from one to the other! Drug running, for sure!

The surveillance aircraft did an immediate sharp bank and turned back at low level, just above the trees, and repeatedly circled our position. Our helicopter pilot was an experienced fellow and he took in the situation at a glance. He fired up his ground to air communications channel and explained to the surveillance aircraft crew what was actually happening. They eventually believed him, but not before they had taken many feet of close-up film. I expect we are still on file somewhere in the Great Canberra Archives.

So we proceeded with our work, and I led my team away from the helicopter into the bush. The first inspection site was about a kilometre away on a compass course of close to 270 degrees. Armed with all our gear we set off, me leading with my aerial photographs, compass and technical equipment. At first the land was devoid of trees, just tussock grassland with bare soil between the tussocks, and we were striding out quite well, discussing recent events. It was probably the bizarre strangeness of the coastal surveillance incident that distracted me, for what followed was quite salutary.

How I became aware of it I do not know, I may not have had my mind on the job, but suddenly, in mid stride, I looked down to see a large fat death adder, motionless, just before me, lying on the bare ground between the tussocks at precisely where I was about to plant my foot, in fact my foot was already descending towards it. Death adders are deadly and can strike with great speed and precision. At that particular time, and given the dynamics of my stride, there was only one spot where I could put my foot, but that spot was already occupied by the snake. Perceiving my dilemma,

I tell you true, in full mid stride, keeping all my composure and aplomb, and with a decent hold upon my compass and aerial photographs, I stepped out double stride.

Now no man can span a stride two metres long no matter how it is sprung upon him, especially when he is just about to plant his foot, but I did. What hidden force had saved me? Did immediate urgent need lend me wings? On reconstruction, I know I didn't deviate from my planned and chosen course, I didn't panic or crash about the scrub, collide with trees and bushes or fall uselessly about, I went ahead with equanimity, but with a double length of stride. I can only hope that the snake was just as frightened as I was, because my tread wouldn't have done it much good either; it would have been very much quid pro quo.

And I tell you what, and now I know it to be true, when disaster's full and fair before you, somehow, you find out what you can really do.

One bad morning

The morning started badly. I arose from my bed urgently needing a pee, and with this in mind, when I put on my shorts I left the zipper down, to save time later on. On my way past the kitchen I thought I would put the jug on for a cup of tea so that it would be on the boil when I returned from my ablutions. Then I opened the garage roller door and trotted out into the yard, aware of significant pressure from within, and with thankful anticipation I unzipped my zip to pee. At least I thought I did. But in my somnambulistic condition I forgot that it was already open, so I'd just zipped it up again, and for the life of me I couldn't work out why I couldn't seem to find the old boy. By the time I worked that one out I was really hopping from one foot to the other, but I solved it, and had my leak.

Relieved, I packed away my gear, and in my haste to return to the kitchen and make my cup of tea I zipped up my shorts with a flourish, but unexpectedly I was met with instant excruciating pain; I had caught a bit of my apparatus in the bloody zip. Now getting a zip down past any obstacle is not easy, and that particular one causes more than a mild grimace. Anyway, after considerable hopping around the yard accompanied by the ritual repeating of certain words and phrases I succeeded, and returned to the kitchen and made my by now much needed cup of tea.

I'd had a bad dream overnight about spiders, and with that still giving me a prickly feeling up my spine I knocked my boots out carefully before I put them on. The boots were outside on the back veranda, but I didn't really expect a spider to be in one of them, there never had been before. I took off my thongs and began to put on my boots. The first boot was clear, no spiders there. But as I lifted up the second one a small lizard rushed out the top of it and leaped into the air in its haste to escape. Imagine my shock and surprise! Half a heart attack later I had my boots on. I was making progress!

Then I had to feed the chooks. No dramas there, it was easy. I mixed the feed and took it to them in their chook house, collected a couple of eggs and went back to the veranda to take my boots off. Boots off, I cast around for my thongs – I couldn't see them anywhere! But I had left them right where I put on my boots! It had to be the bloody dog! I was wandering around looking for them, muttering darkly, when something caught my eye, and dimly, after some seconds of observation my mind twigged; I was holding my thongs in my other hand! I must have picked them up absent mindedly when I sat down to take off my boots. It looked like being a long day.

By this time, visions were running around my head of other times, like when I thought I had lost my glasses and sought my second pair, only to discover that I couldn't wear two pairs at once; trying to take off my singlet whilst I still had my hat on; and once when I was asked what time it was at a bit of a booze-up, turning my wrist over to read my watch and pouring my glass of beer over my feet. Surely it wasn't going to turn out to be one of those days? But it was. What confirmed my suspicion was when I saw an interesting bird down on the bird feeder and picked up my binoculars to have a closer look. As I went to put the binoculars down again, I found myself wondering "how do you turn these damn things off?"

Refreshed after my cup of tea, I hopped into the car to nip down to the corner store and get a morning newspaper to read whilst I was having breakfast. It was still quite early, and the sun was low in the morning sky and shining inconveniently into my eyes, so I turned down the interior visor for protection. You wouldn't believe it, as I did so a huge huntsman spider fell from behind it with a soggy thud right into my crotch, and enraged, proceeded to thrash about until it found a footing in that already sensitized personal area, then it shot down my leg and vanished somewhere underneath the dashboard. I stopped waving my arms wildly in its direction, and steadying the car as best I could, I regained the correct side of the road. You hear of these things happening but never imagine they will happen to you, certainly not all at once.

I bought my newspaper and proceeded back towards home, thinking that this really was turning out to be a bugger of a morning. Even the headlines looked bad. Somewhat frazzled, I pulled out a cigarette and lit it, hoping to calm my nerves. Fine. Then as I swung the wheel to turn into my driveway, I accidentally knocked my cigarette and the butt fell right there, you know where, to aggravate matters still further. Now that hurt, the butt was burning hot and right on that already offended part. After colliding gently with the wheelbarrow, I managed to stop the car and disembark, and divest myself of that flaming butt.

Safely back at home nature called, as it does most mornings, so I sought and sat upon the toilet seat. Now I had used this toilet many times and was quite used to keeping Percy off the porcelain at the front. But this time I had a shock! In my still bemused state, I became aware that Percy had encountered "something" right at his leading edge. At first I was amazed, what was this? I knew this toilet well, there wasn't supposed to be anything there, in that spot. Suddenly, visions of red-back spiders, green frogs and tree snakes hit me, and I hastily vacated the seat to reconnoiter. It was the bloody "toilet fresh" thing; it had moved around to the front.

The only thing that stopped me from calling it a day and going back to bed was the thought of getting up again, and the question of how much more of this my old boy could really stand!

I hate lawn mowers

I guess most of us have a lawn and need to mow it, and maybe quite a lot of people like their lawn mowers and get on quite well with them. I have always hated lawn mowers, especially those stupid little popping ones that rev so mindlessly on Sundays in suburbia. I'm sure that it's mutual, because I know now that lawn mowers hate me too. They work OK for other people, starting meekly and running smoothly, never failing or calling it a day. But for me, they automatically turn on all their vice. I know lawn mowers.

I was going to make one of my own once, an infallible, never fail, last-forever, obedient lawn mower. I was going to buy a Vicon triple bladed agricultural hay mower disk and a five horsepower Honda engine and mount them on something like a horizontal motorbike and be done with it. But even that proved difficult; it was almost as though these simple parts knew they were to become a lawn mower and refused to cooperate and be built. So in the end I bought a "Big Bob".

For a while, that was the end of my problem. Whilst that mower was new it worked flawlessly, and I began to feel that a sort of curse had been lifted. I became quite cocky and began to really enjoy mowing my lawn. I had a system. First, sink a couple or so cans of beer. Then, do an emu parade and clear the lawn of items not to be mowed. It was quite a big lawn, but not so bad really because out of 75 acres I only had to mow about half an acre, the cattle did the rest.

The machine started on the first or second pull of the cord. Then, do you know what I used to do? I set the thing at absolutely full throttle just short of the choke, took a good hold on the handles and faced that lawn, square on. I reckoned that the slow suburban walk was half my trouble, you had to dominate and control these mowers, they had to know who was boss. A few deep breaths, then with a primal scream, hurling invectives at the thing, I launched forth upon the job, at the run. Galloping around in a semi-demented frenzy, with blue smoke and kikuyu grass going everywhere, I mowed that lawn. There were bits of heavy going but I wasn't going to slow down and give the thing a chance to quit, so I jacked the Big Bob back on its rear wheels, and with a few pirouettes, went over those bits again. The only near neighbours were my cattle and some pythons, but thank goodness, they knew me already.

Then the rot set in. My new mower began to phase itself out. I didn't know whether the kikuyu grass was too much for it or there was something wrong with the fuel. The mower people who sold it to me thought it was the fuel. Mind you, I didn't tell them about my methodology! The thing that was happening was that a little ball of lead would form and grow between the electrodes of the spark plug and short it out, and as quickly as I cleaned the plug and got it going it would do it again, and time and time again it just kept on doing this. The fuel companies were mucking about with their octane ratings at the time, and the mower salesman insisted it was probably their fault. No! I knew what it was. That bloody mower had worked me out and had systematically set about a failure profile; it had begun to hate me.

Things really went from bad to worse. The time came when I would approach the thing carefully, whistling nonchalantly, from downwind even so that it couldn't smell me coming, and then grab it, give it a quick cuff to go on with, offer a selection of dire imprecations, and set about my "tirade and start" procedure once again. Sometimes it worked, but in the end I just gave up, and the whole debacle descended into a pathetic futile wrestling match.

One day when I was a bit short of cool I went and got the thing and tried to start it, but it wouldn't go. Overcome by fury at this ungrateful stupid idiotic sham of a bloody mowing machine I grabbed it in my hands and in impotent wrath I threw it into the back of my vehicle, and in high dudgeon took it to the local tip. The tip was burning at the time and I threw it into the biggest flames that I could find, and stood there and watched it burn. I had the last laugh; that would teach it to hate me!

And that, I thought, was that. What I didn't know was that some mowers seem to have a life after death, and this one came back to haunt me. I suspect that my lawn had formed a sort of alliance with that mower, because it began to grow, rank and fast, full of weeds, and I had visions of it rising up and completely engulfing the house. In total resignation I called in a contractor to mow it, and as though it was in the hands of someone who understood it, my lawn has behaved itself ever since.

Bloody lawn mowers!

Invasion by feral pigs

Against my advice, we were camped on a waterhole. Young men always like to camp on water. You can tell them until you are blue in the face, "No, not on water". Go there by all means, have a wash and fill the water tanks, but then go back out to a nice dry ridge and camp there. On that ridge there are no mosquitoes, no crocodiles, no scrub bulls coming down to drink, and best of all no feral pigs. But this time it was three to one and the young men had their way, and we camped beside that waterhole. It was quite a nice spot really, full of trees and shrubs, shady places, birds, even some grass. But it was a waterhole.

It was towards the end of the dry season and the waterhole had lost a lot of water, it now had wide, muddy margins, and there were two half-starved cattle bogged there in the mud. One of them seemed to have been bogged for only a short time and we were able to pull it out by tying a rope around its horns and gently hauling with one of the Toyotas. The other one had clearly been there for some time and was certainly going to die before we got it out, or at any rate soon after. In fact, I shot it. I shot it because the feral pigs had found it on their nightly foray down to the water and had eaten some of its guts out whilst it was still alive, probably over the preceding few days. Pigs aren't nice animals, whatever those who keep pet ones might think. We pulled the carcass out to prevent it from polluting the remaining water.

Near the waterhole, we dragged in some firewood and made a good camp, the two vehicles spaced a little apart with a nice flat area between them where the cook had his folding table and a kerosene pressure lamp to work with, and we all had room to sit down with our pannikins of tea. The fire was lit well out in front of the vehicles. Dinner was beginning to smell pretty good and we were immersed in our yarns, when we heard a sound from the direction of the waterhole. It was the unmistakable squealing, grunting sound of feral pigs, coming in to drink at the waterhole. They were also going to feast on the remains of the stricken beast, which mercifully was now dead. I remembered another sound one often hears at night. The last time I heard that one was in the Victoria River district. It sounded exactly like a lion roaring, and one member of my team was quite convinced that it was. He thought that a lion must have escaped from some circus and that we were in dire potential danger. But I knew what it was, it was only a Brahman bull, grumbling along towards water.

But pigs are pigs wherever you find them, especially feral pigs, and this lot was no exception. They must have caught the smell of our dinner cooking, for they suddenly invaded our camp. The whole mob of them just appeared amongst us, trotting quickly into our camp kitchen, grunting and squealing, twitching their noses in search of our food. But then they smelt and saw us, and their almost instinctive search for food instantly turned to fear, and when a pig gets frightened it immediately becomes defensive and aggressive, and they went berserk. We reacted immediately, for a boar's tusks are at a very dangerous height for men, and none of us were keen to go hands on with a feral pig anyway. We did the only thing we could, we shot up onto the tops of the vehicles.

Then those pigs embarked upon a demolition rampage. In their fear and fright, they wrecked our camp; the table, chairs, the food, all in one moment were tusked and thrown about, and instant pandemonium and catastrophe prevailed. Now luckily the vehicle I was on top of was mine, and it contained my rifle, standing just inside the door. By lying on my stomach on the roof I could just reach down inside the open window and secure it. Fortunately, it was full of ammunition and had a spare magazine. Then I had to check where everybody was, for it is a cardinal bush rule never to fire a rifle when in camp at night unless all members of your party are present and accounted for, because that noise out there may be one of your party relieving himself. That done, from my rooftop perch I shot every pig I saw, probably some of them twice, for they were milling around in panic, and probably some of them not at all, but not one of them fell that I could see. Surely, I wasn't that bad a shot? But they got the message and left our camp, with the goodness to leave the devastated remains of our dinner behind them.

Next morning, I counted five dead pigs in the grass around our camp. I think there was some good in it though, for I never knew any of those young blokes camp on water again.

Rogue feral buffalo

I've had several contretemps with buffalo. These are feral animals, quite recently introduced to Australia from nearby Asia, and before the bulk of them were shot or domesticated they were responsible for a lot of environmental damage. There aren't many wild buffalo left now, but when they were there in large numbers they were mostly fairly placid and retiring, especially when they congregated in large herds on the open coastal plains east of Darwin. Individuals, however, such as old bulls cast out from the herd could be quite cranky and aggressive.

There aren't many rogue female buffaloes, they get killed by the bulls. When the older or sicker cows come into season, which they can't help, and the bull tries to mount them, they collapse under his weight, and the bull gores them to death in his efforts to get them up again. It's the same with outback cattle.

A friend of mine near the small settlement of Noonamah south of Darwin had a pet buffalo, a bull. It was a boisterous sort of relationship, the buffalo being strong and well fed, and inclined to play rather vigorously with anything that came to hand, including its owner, if it could. Not your normal Siamese cat I guess, but my friend was a big strong fellow and coped well with his pet. Eventually my friend felt that his buffalo needed something other than himself to occupy its mind, so he gave him an old car body to play with. The buffalo was delighted, and used to roll this old vehicle over and around his paddock for hours at a time.

There had been some roadwork on the Stuart Highway nearby and the Works Department staff had asked my friend if they could park some of their equipment on the side of his driveway to ensure its safety at night. Of course, he agreed, and for some days this worked very well. Then came Friday, and the only machine that the roads people wanted to leave there that weekend was a large, almost new Broomwade compressor. The roadwork men were very considerate and wanted to leave my friend's driveway as clear as possible for the weekend, so they opened a nearby gate and parked the compressor in one of his paddocks. What they didn't know was that it was the pet buffalo's paddock!

Wow! thought the buffalo, when he came to the gate and saw it. A new toy to play with! A big bright yellow car body! So he proceeded to roll it around the paddock. I don't think the Works Department were too impressed on the next

Monday morning when they were trying to work out how to retrieve the thing, because the buffalo wasn't giving up his new toy without a fight. In the end, they decoyed him by pretending to steal his original toy, the old car body, and whilst he was busy defending that, they hitched up what was left of the compressor and drove away with it. That buffalo wasn't really a rogue, he was just young and enthusiastic.

There certainly were some bad ones though. In those days we used the old FJ45 Toyotas for our fieldwork, and they were a sort of blueish-grey colour. Ours were very close to buffalo colour, due to the weathering of the paint in the sun and accumulated increments of dust and mud. We were surveying in two of these vehicles in the Daly Basin on Claravale Station one day, completely off road, when we came to a nice green flat area in the bend of a creek. It was almost treeless but well grassed, and the waterhole in the creek was permanent. I had in mind that it would make a nice place for our morning smoko, and so I headed towards a large shady tree near the bank of the creek. What I didn't know but was very soon to find out was that one of those old cast-out buffalo bulls had migrated to this place and made it his home, and he was now the owner and boss of that creek flat. This old bull was not a happy fellow, quite cantankerous in fact, and when he saw us he must have thought that our vehicle was another buffalo, come to disturb him in his peace, and possibly steal his home and land and move him on. Without hesitation, he charged. Now we were in a quandary because we were in the bush in low range and not travelling very fast, but I can tell you that as soon as we saw this fellow coming we hit high range in the Toyotas, and regardless of terrain we shot up through the gears and high-tailed it out of there. That one was definitely a rogue.

Out on the open coastal plains there were also rogue old bulls, but they seemed less inclined to be aggressive. There was a time when the CSIRO was doing a reconnaissance survey of the soils on these coastal plains, and the soil scientist concerned was later to become my boss in Darwin, which was when I heard this story. The work was being done using a helicopter for transport, as the plains were wet and impassable to vehicles at that time. My boss and one assistant were dropped off at a spot on the plains, miles from any of the higher forested land, to auger out and describe a soil profile, which would take about an hour. The helicopter left them and returned to the base camp to refuel. All around was open clay plain, except for one small tree nearby. In some apprehension, for this was prime buffalo country, the two men started work, keeping watch all the while for any sign of buffalo.

Then, incredibly, from a muddy wallow not fifty metres from them, there stood up one large old bull buffalo. Why the helicopter had not spooked him is impossible to know, but now, there he was, larger than life, eyeing the two men off with a look of considerable distaste. We will never know for sure what passed through their minds at that particular moment because the story was embellished and exaggerated considerably later that evening back in camp, but I do know that they at once took stock of that small tree. I think they reached consensus quite rapidly; the tree was quite inadequate, and there was no way they could outrun that buffalo; their only recourse if it charged them would be to wave things about and shout and try to bluff it out. So they continued working, nervously hoping that the helicopter would return sooner rather than later. I guess also that neither of them relished the prospect of being found halfway up that spindly plant when the helicopter did return, especially if there were spectators with cameras in the helicopter when it arrived. Fortunately for them, the buffalo stayed put and they didn't have to test the tree. Or was it unfortunately, because they were well and truly photographed when the helicopter did come back to pick them up!

I'll bet they were pleased though that this particular buffalo was only an amateur rogue.

Palmer at Douglas River

If one spends a lot of time in the bush one comes across all sorts of drivers. I knew a couple of beauties.

I met one bush driver whose vehicle had no roof. He would stand or rather squat upon the driver's seat, grip the steering wheel firmly for balance and proceed like a jockey in his stirrups; he reckoned he got a better view that way, and could bail out quickly if necessary. He used the hand throttle instead of the accelerator pedal and could change gears without using the clutch, so he got along quite well. He didn't have much time for brakes, but then he only ever drove in the bush. Another one really hated black soil plains; he found them easier to walk across than drive over because those plains are very rough, so he would put his vehicle in low gear and get out and walk along beside it, steering with an occasional arm through the window. But of all of them I have to say that the most consistently bad was my old boss in Darwin. He could wreck a vehicle anywhere, anytime, he didn't even need to be in the bush. I never met a driver quite as predictably bad as Palmer.

We'd been out bush in the Daly Basin for a couple of weeks, four of us in two Toyota Land Cruisers, doing land assessment work. Our boss Toby Palmer had come out to see us, ostensibly to check on the progress of the work but really because he just liked to escape from the office and get out into the bush for a while. This time he had a valid excuse, for we were operating in an area accessible for his vehicle (only marginally, he had a Ford Falcon station wagon), and also because others of our team were setting up a field day for local farmers in the Douglas River catchment a bit further to the north and he was going to participate in it. So he came down to visit us.

Toby had with him a soil scientist from the CSIRO in Canberra who was keen to see the country, and we in turn were keen to ask his opinion on the land and its capabilities. As I was team leader and wanted to be in the discussion between him and Palmer, I left my Land Cruiser to one of my men and joined them in the Falcon station wagon. We still had a way to go to get to the field day site.

Now Palmer loved to drive around the bush but unfortunately, he wasn't very good at it, and a Falcon station wagon was not the best vehicle to do it with. He crashed and bounded around the scrub, across rocks and gullies, all amiss, until eventually the CSIRO chap removed his pipe and laconically said, "Toby, would you like me to drive it?" But never bested, Toby treated that as jest, for he knew where he was going, and he bounded on towards the Douglas River, and erratically, in classic Palmer style we progressed towards our destination.

At this point I need to tell you something of a story. Toby had come from the DSIR, the Kiwi equivalent of Australia's CSIRO, to work with the CSIRO in the Division of Soils on Black Mountain in Canberra, and he was liked and very well regarded there, professionally and personally. It was there that an appellation concerning him was promulgated. I do not know this for sure, I was not there, I heard it from my colleagues. There was a time at a conference of scientists where he was delivering a talk, and unlike him, he failed to make the grade, stuffed up in every possible way, committed borborygmi, and respected as he was, the meeting was rendered silent, all aghast, no-one could speak, or knew what ought be done to retrieve the situation. But one was there, an astute and quick-thinking man, the chairman of the meeting, and he paused a moment, then came up to the platform. And slowly and deliberately he said, "You are now participating in another Palmer cock-up. There will be no extra charge, only the needle will be changed to protect the record". It was, as I understand it, a completely spontaneous response, and I think an erudite and compassionate one, it preserved everybody's dignity, the integrity of science, and turned disaster into mirth.

There was another one, too. There was a store-cum-pub well out west of Darwin on the old Arnhem Highway in the South Alligator Rivers region, owned and run by a friend of Toby's. I was there with him once; he was at that time a CSIRO soils scientist, ostensibly on a work mission but in reality, to fish. We spent some time in the pub talking to the owner and imbibing beer. Then my boss decided that he had better do the job he came there for, which was to describe a soils pit that had recently been dug for him to inspect. So off he went to find his pit. Unfortunately, he chose the wrong pit; he began to describe the face of a disused toilet pit, instead of the newly opened one that had been dug for him. That was the origin of the saying about him that as a soil scientist, he couldn't tell shit from clay.

Anyway, on this occasion we finally emerged from the bush and pulled in at the Adelaide River pub on the Stuart Highway. We hadn't had a beer for weeks, so it was some time later that we hit the road again, Palmer in his Falcon wagon, the CSIRO chap with him, and the rest of us now back in our four wheel drives. Then Toby hit a cow, broke its neck and killed it. The cow had just emerged from the roadside scrub and ambled straight into Toby's path and he hit it with his left front mudguard, crumpled it and smashed the headlight. His car was damaged once again. He was known for this and had been warned, he was a shocking driver. He sat there behind the wheel quietly reciting, damn, damn, damn, etcetera (read the vernacular into that). But he could still drive it, so we pulled the dead cow off the road and proceeded to our destination, beside the Douglas River.

When we arrived at the river the field day was well advanced, and had apparently gone very well, with much interest from the farmers; there were about twenty of them. We had a tray-back truck that we'd used to show them round our sites, with bales of hay on the tray to use as seats. This was different country from that in the south of Australia and could not be safely farmed in the same way, and that message had clearly gotten through and been accepted.

Then it was the end of the field day tour, and lunch time. We had planned to finish the field day in a nice spot on a beautiful stretch of the Douglas River, and to provide a really good barbeque style lunch for the farmers who were there. We pulled the truck up on solid ground just beside the steeply sloping riverbank, and the farmers disembarked. They had to walk down the bank, as it was far too steep for normal vehicles. Then we in our four-wheel drives drove carefully down that riverbank to help our fellow staff, because our cook and crew had a full bush barbeque prepared down there, on a grassy flat just beside the water. There was a large campfire, billys boiling, and buffalo fillet, barramundi, damper, onions and chilies, condiments and sauces, all of it laid out there and waiting.

Then suddenly came Palmer, with his usual bound, in his Falcon station wagon. And down the Douglas Riverbank he came, in that fearful wagon, in second gear, directly down the slope, and straight towards the river at hopeless speed he went. He roared right down that riverbank, closing fast upon the water, we stopped and looked, he'd never make it, with brakes all locked, he was almost in the river. But undaunted, Toby pulled it out just before the water, and on full lock, leaning hard, wheels scrabbling, he raced around the corner. And he shot it right across the fire, straight through the barbeque and fish and meat and damper and down along the grassy river flat, and some way past the camp he brought it to a halt.

The cook was Polish, generally a placid chap, but apt to imbibe a little now and then to help him concentrate. This had been his big day; he was on display, now he could show what he could really do as a bush cook. It was interesting to observe the changes that came over the cook as his beautiful creations, so lovingly prepared, were bashed into oblivion. At first, he was amazed, then incredulous, then definitely unimpressed, and as the full horror of what had happened to his barbeque dawned upon him he grew quite excited. The food was still raining down from almost treetop height, the campfire looked as though it had been ploughed, and a small grass fire had kindled off there to the right. The barbeque itself had left the scene; it was now attached to the front of Palmer's wagon. Poor cook! But it was when a large piece of buffalo steak came whistling past his ear and simultaneously an almost empty billy can clanged down upon his left shoulder that he really began to take umbrage.

Then twenty farmers and half a dozen of our staff were treated to part two of the spectacle. The cook just went berserk. He grabbed bits of meat and damper and stomped violently upon them, threw them in the river and at anyone he saw, vigorously scattered his pots and pans around the bush, and all the while he screamed and yelled in Polish with the odd foray into the Australian bush vernacular, during which he quit several times, outlined a couple of ancestries, and made liberal with Palmer's curriculum vitae. I think the farmers enjoyed it more than they would have the meal, and I'm sure some of them thought that we had put it on especially, as a kind of show.

Palmer meanwhile had emerged from his wagon, his feelings quite sublime, and nonchalantly smiled. Then the Canberra CSIRO chap came out from in the wagon, his eyes agog, he'd never had a ride quite like it. As for our staff, I think that what was in their minds were the old prophetic words; "You are now participating in another Palmer cock-up. There will be no extra charge, only the needle will be changed to protect the record".

Annual sorghum
– a grass that moves

There are always new things to find out in the bush and some of them are quite amazing. I may be a slow learner, but eventually I discovered a couple of interesting things about the most common grass in the Northern Territory Top End, annual sorghum (Sorghum stipoideum).

We were working in the Daly Basin, south of Darwin. The task before us was to describe and map the land resources of several large adjoining cattle properties. Amongst other things, we wanted to find areas where more intensive agriculture could be viable. In those days, there were very few roads and we "scrub-bashed" through the bush in four-wheel drive vehicles, navigating with the aid of aerial photographs. At night we just camped out in the bush, mostly right where we finished work. Our main requirements for a good camp site were an ironwood tree with dry fallen branches, for that was good, hot, smoke-free firewood, and with it, an open area where we could roll out our swags and have room to light a fire and cook our evening meal. Sometimes we navigated to a more pleasant spot, perhaps to an un-burnt, less rocky, or a flatter area, or maybe a riverbank. We had to be quite self-sufficient; we had all our food, our swags, and enough fuel and water to last.

Much of that country had annual sorghum as its main grass, and at this time of year the grass was mature and dry and had already set its seed, and the seeds had fallen prolifically to the ground. Annual sorghum seeds are long and pointy like all spear grasses, a bit like oats, and they have a large awn, set at an angle to the axis of the seed. This awn is not straight, but in the form of a spiral, and it is very responsive to moisture. When wet it absorbs moisture and the spiral unwinds, and as this happens the awn turns around the seed in an arc. Because the awn is set at an angle, as it turns it catches on bits of stick, or grass, or stones and becomes immobilized, and then the seed attached to it turns around instead, and as it does so it bores down a little into the soil. Then, as it dries, the spiral in the awn curls up again, the awn turns back and catches once more on an obstacle so that the seed is given another turn but in the opposite direction, and so on, back and forth, until the seed bores right down into the soil. Backward-facing bristles prevent it coming out again. At this time of year, the moisture is supplied by night-time dew which dries up again with day-time heat, so the seeds have many cycles of wetting and drying to bury themselves in the soil, like a sort of self-planting grass. Thus the seeds are safe from ants and fire, and assured of soil moisture from the early rains of the next wet season.

Now on that particular day I had two run-ins with annual sorghum. The first time, I had moved aside from the work area to relieve myself. As I pissed, my mind in neutral, I became aware of a gentle rustling sound, which grew more urgent as I listened. Fearing that it was a snake I hastily scanned my surroundings, but there was nothing unusual to be seen. Perhaps it was just the sound of falling piss. But the sound continued after I had finished, which made me jump back in alarm. As I did so I looked down at where I had just wet the ground, and saw the "dead" grass moving, writhing there before my eyes in an altogether inexplicable fashion, and the rustling sound was coming from it. Surely my piss couldn't have been that toxic? I looked more closely, and it was then that I discovered the secret of the awns. They were just responding naturally to getting wet!

The second run-in was later that night. We had camped out under the stars, miles from anywhere. We'd had our meal, a nice one too, of beef and mashed potato. We'd had a yarn, and drank some tea, and looked forward to our bedtime because we'd had a full-on day, and by the end of it we were tired. We unrolled our swags, and yawning, prepared to get aboard them, intent upon our sleep. The campfire was dying down and we were in our swags and dosing off to sleep, listening to the music of the bush – a dingo howling its eerie, yearning song, the wailing of a curlew, a scrub bull calling in the far distance, plus of course the insects, and all the little creaks and snaps of the night, and those strange muted sounds one cannot place.

But sleep was not to be had, at least not for me, because there came a noise I did not know, a curious rustling sound, and it was coming from all around our camp, including from just beside my swag. The men were all asleep, and half asleep myself, I lay inside my swag listening to this noise. I had no idea what it was, but it was clearly coming from the ground. As I lay there, I invoked all my science and logic, determined to discover what was producing it, whilst that peculiar rustle just continued on. Curious, I turned on my torch to get some light and had a good look around, but there was nothing there, all was as it should be. There were no animals, no fire, no wind, and it couldn't have been a snake because it was coming from everywhere, right across our camping area. Surely it couldn't be the annual sorghum seeds, it was still far too hot for there to be any dew to wet the awns. But just to check, I shone my torch upon the ground, which was covered in a shallow litter of dead annual sorghum, all of it quite still and flat. But then I saw the dead grass moving; for the second time that day, the dry remains of the annual sorghum were gently twitching on the ground. I looked more closely, and discovered that the whole surface of the soil was covered with a species of termite, grass eaters, and they were cutting up the dry sorghum stems into short manageable lengths of about a centimetre and taking them underground to their "larder" to store and use as food until the next year's opportunity came to do it again, hence that rustling sound. It seems they emerge from down inside the ground at night to gather in their crop, and this was their annual harvest time.

So for the second time that day I saw and heard the annual sorghum move, but this time for an entirely different reason. What a grass! So back to the calling of the dingo, and some much-needed sleep!

Kangaroo stew or bush turkey?

We'd been out bush for three weeks, more or less, all of it off road, on a soil survey job on Oolloo and Jindare Stations. But towards the end of this particular trip our diet had begun to get a bit repetitive; it had degenerated into being always just bloody kangaroo.

In those days we didn't have vehicle refrigerators and all our perishable food had to be packed into iceboxes. We used to put dry ice on top of the ordinary ice in one icebox and seal it, and if we used its contents last; it would still be reasonably cold after three days or so out in the bush. After that second icebox ran out we were on tinned food, or whatever we could procure from the bush. We shot the odd duck or a passably decent kangaroo, or caught fish, we had some excellent black bream at times. And then there were the lizards if you could catch them; the blue tongues were the best.

Our bush cook at the time wasn't all that hot. His ducks weren't too good because he used to just gut and pluck them roughly and then chop them into pieces, bones and all, and boil the resulting mess. He was also pretty bad on warmed up tinned tucker, he managed to make nameless slime out of it every time. But on kangaroo he was really awful. Towards the end of this trip most of what we got was luke-warm half raw kangaroo stew. We used to shoot one, just one at a time because there were so many, and we had no need to hoard. We'd skin the back of the top part, then cut the rest of the top half of the body off at the waist and throw it away. Then we would wrap the haunches in the skin flap from the back, and to secure it we cut a hole in this flap of skin and poked the tail through. Then we tied this package of kangaroo "rump" to the scrub bar of one of the vehicles and scrub bashed with it for a day or two to knock the vermin off and allow it to become a bit more tender. More kangaroo stew! Being half raw was not too bad; thankfully it was only occasionally that it was a little bit rotten. By this time the remains of our bread were so dry and hard we used to crack pieces of it off by smacking it with the back of an axe on the tailboard of one of the vehicles; we preferred damper. The tucker was not very good.

To make matters worse, that evening we couldn't find a decent spot to camp. My team had worked hard and looked forward to a pleasant spot, preferably near water, or at least a grassy clearing with firewood close at hand. But all around was burnt, as were many places at the end of the dry season, and we were stuck in a most desolate spot. We had plenty of firewood but there was no grass and no water, all around was ashes, and we knew the ash would blow right through the vehicles and even track into our swags.

We set up camp as best we could, cooked our meal, and climbed into our swags. I couldn't sleep, but then I remembered something. That night there was to be an eclipse of the moon when the sun, the earth and the moon would be in alignment, and we were well placed to see it, clear skies too. So I waited, more content, until it started, and I saw it all from snug inside my swag, The moon was full, it slowly dulled, as the great arc of the earth's shadow consumed it. The dingoes and the curlews, in consternation, lapsed into silence. At its peak the moon was fully covered, just a circular hint of hidden light where it had been. Then the moon emerged again but from the other side, and slowly came back to the full. It all seemed incongruous to me, our blackened moonscape for a campsite, a lunar eclipse, and the dingoes and the curlews crying out again.

Next day we finished our work and were making our way through the bush towards a formed road, the township of Pine Creek, and "civilization". Then – we all saw them at the same time – two big fat bush turkeys (plains bustards) were slowly stalking by, quite close. They were not protected in those days, we were hungry, and bush turkeys are delicious! Without anybody saying a word, the vehicles pulled down to a halt, and from each vehicle one man slowly emerged, took a rifle, aimed carefully, and in synchronized accord (I know not how), they fired. They were making no mistake, and two bush turkeys fell. All activity immediately stopped, we plucked and gutted the turkeys, salivating at the prospect of a decent feed at last. Then we drove through the bush on compass course directly to Pine Creek, bugger looking for the road. First, of course, we went to the pub, to wet our whistles and recover our composure and aplomb, then to Ah Toy's, the most interesting and varied general store ever, where we bought some food and more grog, and then we drove on out of town.

I knew a place to camp, on the top of a shingly hill. I knew that it was possible to get there, I had camped up there before. There was a reasonably flat spot up on top able to accommodate three vehicles if we placed them around the edges, plus space for several men to camp. There was always a good breeze up there and no mosquitoes, crocodiles or feral pigs – a perfect place. Sure, there was a dry creek to cross at the bottom and that was fairly wild, but again it was possible. And so we crawled our way up there in bottom gear low range, careful to stay square on to the slope, arranged ourselves, and pitched camp.

We found my old campfire straight away, collected a pile of firewood, cranked up the cook with a good slosh of OP rum and spread out our swags. We had a couple more beers (except the cook! - more rum for him), and then the cook produced the finest roast dinner anyone could ever desire. This was not half raw kangaroo. The two roast turkeys, the last of our sweet potatoes, some carrots and parsnips and two left-over tins of peas and bully beef were all roasted to perfection. What a change, what a lovely spot, what a challenge to get to it, such good food and such good company, all of them good bushmen!

And I had discovered something, and I made a mental note to put rum on the shopping list for our next trip. Because the cook was quite OK, a very good cook really, but not when he was sober; and he had confessed, he didn't like half raw kangaroo either!

A contrast in fishing techniques

Fishing stories certainly provoke tall tales about the one that got away, and produce hotly contested assertions concerning which lure or bait is the best for which fish in whatever kind of water or weather conditions. Fishermen will talk for hours about fishing.

But I've not yet heard of a contrast in fishing techniques quite like this one. Let me tell you about it. It occurred to me whilst I was landing a big barramundi one day that there are all sorts of ways to catch a fish. This was actually one of them, a "technique" I made up as I went along. I was camped on Anwoollolla Lagoon, south of Tipperary homestead on the road to the old Beeboom Crossing on the Daly River. We'd caught a few fish, but they were quite "muddy" to taste, and a lot got thrown back. Then I snagged a big one and was desperate to land it and find out how big it was.

Now this barramundi didn't behave as usual. It dragged like a dead weight in the water, rather than rushing about and leaping out of the water as they usually do. I pulled it in to shore, but there was no way I could get it out, it was just too big. I called for help, and my friend came and held the line while I cut down a thin sapling with a nice "V" in one of its branches. This sapling was about two metres long, with a small branch forming a sort of hook near one end. By catching the hook in the fish's gills, I finally managed to drag it out. That is actually true, that is how I landed it. It weighed in at 25 kilograms, not so big really, but still a nice fish.

What were we to do with it now? It was sure to be muddy, like all the rest. We were about to leave the lagoon at that time and return to Darwin, so I thought it would be a nice gesture to give this fish to the Tipperary station manager, who had very kindly allowed us to camp and fish there. He would have known it would be muddy and just passed it on after I had given it to him, but it was a traditional sort of gesture and he accepted it in the spirit of things. Nice bloke, that.

Another time I was in my four metre tinnie with outboard power on a large lagoon called Jim-Jim Waterhole, on the old road to the East Alligator River crossing. The place was later referred to as Cooinda when a store and bar were built there. But back to the tinnie. We were trolling for barramundi, and there were plenty of big ones there. It was a beautiful lagoon, flanked by big paperbarks, Leichardt pines, pandanus palms and scrambling vines. The boat was cruising along at low to idle revs on the outboard and I had payed out a good strong hand-held line with a red wobbler lure on a strong trace. These red wobblers were hinged in the middle and had two triple hooks, one hung from the centre pivot and one at the rear. We had found them to be deadly on barra, and once again that soon proved to be the case.

I had to make an adjustment to the engine which needed both my hands, so I wrapped the line around the next most prehensile appendage, my big toe, then leaned towards the rear of the boat and proceeded with the adjustment. Wouldn't you know it, a barra chose that moment to strike the lure, and the line jerked out and tightened on my big toe. Now barra are highly active game fish and this was a big one, and the pain in my toe was excruciating. True to type, and as though mocking me for my unpreparedness, it leapt high out of the water trying to rid itself of the hook at the end of a very taut line, in classic barra style. My big toe was up at the other end of the boat, and the barra seemed intent on pulling me out of the boat and into the water, or removing my toe altogether. I had no intention of leaving the boat at that time as this lagoon was home to some very large crocodiles. With some difficulty, I managed to grope my way down there and grab hold of the line in a more conventional manner. Thus secured, after a long fight I eventually landed that fish, but my big toe was all but ring-barked and remained sore for weeks. I coped with this quite well philosophically, for it had long been my contention that if you haven't broken yourself up a bit during life then you haven't been really trying.

I was also partial to black bream, and in complete contrast to my barramundi fishing episode I used a different method to fish for them, that's if you could call the barra on my big toe event a "method". I knew of a small waterhole in an isolated part of the Daly Basin on Oolloo Station. We were mapping land near there and at intervals we would pass this spot, and never missed an opportunity to catch some bream for dinner. The water hole was just a crevice in a limestone rock outcrop in the bed of a small creek, not an obvious place, with only a couple of Tristania trees, some small paperbarks and a few pandanus palms around to identify it. I had found it initially on aerial photographs and navigated there on purpose to find out why that frontage vegetation was there, for the creek itself was relatively insignificant and at that time quite dry. Imagine our amazement when we found this small waterhole full of juicy fat black bream! The water in the crevice was crystal clear, smooth and unruffled on the surface, and the bream could be seen quite clearly just idling in the shady parts of the hole, and sometimes drifting lazily about. Now this has got to be the simplest way to catch a fish ever. All we had to do was bait a little hook with a grub or piece of meat and lower it straight down in front of a fish's mouth. The fish would contemplate this offering for a few moments, and then obligingly just swallow the bait. They didn't even struggle when we pulled them out, two or three of them in five minutes.

No sport in that, you say, but it was a lot easier on my big toe!

Attack by water buffalo

Maybe we are all a bit wary of feral buffalo and feel that they could attack at any moment, and when one is exposed to a mob of them in a compromising situation this is a very real feeling.

We were approaching a lagoon. Like all these Top End coastal plain lagoons it was a beautiful place. It was a large lagoon, some 200 metres across, shallow at the edges where the water lilies grew, but the open water in the middle was deep and clear. A gently sloping sandy beach surrounded it, the upper limits of which marked the wet season water line. Surrounding the whole lagoon was a broad band of tall paperbark trees, and outside that, an endless open savannah of short scrubby trees and coarse grass. We wanted to visit that savannah as part of the sampling we were doing for a regional soil survey, and the best landing spot for our helicopter was on the sandy margin of the lagoon.

As we had expected, the water and much of the beach were alive with water birds; Jabiru storks, Magpie geese, Burdekin ducks, spoonbills, Jesus birds (leaf runners), moorhens, herons, kingfishers and many more. We buzzed the site, this lovely spot, to rouse and fly the birds, because airborne birds are a real hazard for helicopters, and we had to clear them before we could land. They rose in clouds with a trail of crap and feathers, and a chaos of ripples on the water. We stayed clear until they had gone; they didn't have far to go, just on to the next lagoon. We landed there, with noise and flurry, violating the natural peace and calmness. We disembarked, and with our survey gear, some water and a rifle we left the lagoon and its margin of tall paperbarks and set out on foot to find our destination in the stunted low scrub outside.

We walked with purpose, keeping to our compass course. Half a kilometre further on we found our spot amidst some quite small trees, a pre-determined site marked on our aerial photographs. We began to drill our augered soil inspection hole and started to do our work.

Then all at once there was a sound, and we looked up, disconcerted, to see a group of water buffalo, charging straight towards us! They were coming from the direction of the lagoon, and following straight down upon our tracks, right behind us!

At first, we were incredulous; then as they rapidly drew near, we concluded that they were intent upon us for disturbance of their private place when we landed in the chopper, and with rage and foul intent were coming down to get us. This was unexpected, to say the least. Quite illogically we panicked, and our legs went into gear before our brains. One man grabbed the rifle, one ran around in circles, but most of us, we headed up, and tried to climb a tree. The trees were short and scrubby. We headed for the nearest one, but we all chose just the one same tree, and four of us, together, all tried to climb that tree.

I'd heard of Charley Chaplin, but never had I seen a team of men, in panic, all trying to climb one tree. Four men frantically climbing up, a foot or two, and crashing down again; running round, colliding, then scrabbling up again, just to crash once more. The rumble of buffalo hooves was rapidly coming closer, and our panic turned to desperation. Set upon with renewed vigour that small tree was violently shaken, twigs were ripped away, branches were broken, and bark began flying off it in all directions.

Then all the men were on the ground, beneath that tree, in total disarray, when we realized that the sound had died away. We were not pursued, there was no harm, it was a false alarm. Those buffalo had been spooked by the landing of our chopper, and all they wanted was to get away.

Our pilot told us later that their attention had been so focused on the helicopter winding down its rotors that they didn't seem to notice us depart on foot, and in running away from that machine they had chosen the easiest path, just as we had.

Looking back, I don't know who was most frightened, us or the buffalo, but if I had my guess, I would say that innocent little tree had the biggest fright of all!

A tiny baby bird

I've had a lot to do with Australian outback bushmen in my time and you can't tell me they are as hard as they seem to be. Sure, they appear to be tough and indestructible, and they are, but in my experience, they mostly have a soft and generous core.

At the time that the Ord River scheme was being set up for irrigation we were undertaking an assessment of the commandable land on the Northern Territory side of the border with Western Australia, and documenting the irrigation potential of the soils. Most of the area was old floodplains with dark, heavy, cracking clay soils which were very difficult to bore into with a soil auger, so we used a power-driven coring tube to take out our soil samples. However, as part of the assessment we had to map a perimeter about a kilometre wide around the edges of the plains. The soils here were very variable, often shallow, rocky, or otherwise difficult to sample and we could not use our power equipment, so we had to use the old hand-operated soil auger.

We were in four-wheel drives, travelling across this perimeter country. We came to one spot we wanted to investigate, set in rough bushland with an assortment of trees, shrubs and grasses, an occasional sandstone outcrop and some open patches. We selected our site and began to auger out a hole to expose a sample of the soil. It was solid going, and some effort was required to bore down to our required depth. But we took our turns and each man did his stint, and we grunted down in that firm soil. We were down more than a metre, and all the men were striving hard to push down even further. It was difficult for the auger man to gain purchase on the ground, and we'd trampled the soil around the auger hole considerably in our efforts.

Then one good man, standing to the side, saw something quite peculiar. Immediately he held out his hand and stopped the man on the auger. He was pointing to the auger hole. We looked where he was pointing and at first saw nothing, then as we searched with better concentration, we all saw it together. There was a tiny little baby bird, prostrate upon the soil, right beside our auger hole.

None of us had seen it, it was amazingly intact, just a tiny little fluffy thing still banded by its youth. Instinctively it crouched, utterly immobile, filled with fear, hiding in the only way it knew, by camouflage and stillness. We'd been trampling all around and over it, oblivious of its presence, yet by some miracle we had not stood upon it. We all stepped back, stopped our work, and thought of how to save it, for had we trod a small step more we might have trampled on it. Then those good men put down their tools and cast about to save it.

These were outback bushmen, strong, sturdy, resilient and hard, they'd been through everything the bush could throw at them. They could do anything that was put before them; no matter how seemingly impossible it might be, these men could do it, they were competent, and they were tough. But now this tiny little baby bird was holding all their full and rapt attention. And one picked up this scrap of life, cringing for survival, and with his mates he gently took it from the auger hole, and in his hard and horny hand he moved it to a safer place. Discussing it, they chose some shade with fallen leaves, and carefully laid it down beside a sheltering tussock of dry grass.

Never take a bushman's heart for stone, for "macho" might not be true. There may dwell within that rough facade a wondrous, gentle, unspoiled soul.

A frog in a cabbage gum

I guess the last thing one would expect to find in an environment that could only be considered harsh would be a frog, happily existing, but it happens, just as little fish and crabs come down in rain at times.

I enjoyed working in the Daly Basin. I had come to know it well, so well that I knew all the trees and shrubs and grasses, and the environmental conditions that each one thrived in. I knew the seasons, too. We refer to only two, the wet and the dry, but the Aborigines had something like a dozen, and my sympathies were with them. It was easy to distinguish a range of subtle changes in the ecology as the seasons evolved, and each tree or grass or ant or wallaby would change its tactics to suit the changing conditions. On this particular day it was well into the dry season, and in another month or so we could expect the first storms of the coming wet. The annual grass fires had long since passed and the ash had blown away, and although the grass had gone there was a new layer of dry leaves and twigs upon the ground, for with increasingly dry conditions the eucalyptus trees shed a large proportion of their canopy as a water saving mechanism.

In this dry and baking-hot environment the plants appeared to be just holding on; every tree was hanging out, just waiting for the rain that was surely on the way. From early morning, the Agile Wallabies were under what shade there was, moving around under the trees with the sun. All was stark and brownish coloured; there was not much green about, and nothing stirred but empty, hot little eddies of wind.

We were working right beside a northern cabbage gum, a bloodwood tree (Corymbia clavigera). These "cabbage" gums carry large round leaves in bunches at the end of twigs, which could by a stretch of the imagination be thought to be a bit like cabbages. These are truly wondrous trees, for before any rain has fallen and the ground is hard and dry, inexplicably, they put on a lush new canopy. The soil, the air, could fry a cabbage there, but these trees get up and grow. In total contrast to the rest of the bush the cabbage tree beside us was resplendent, green and lush, with its brand-new canopy of leaves. We wondered, how do they do it? How can these trees produce a succulent new set of leaves, when all around is so harsh and dry? All the other trees were still like scarecrows, almost devoid of leaves, retaining just a few old half dead ones, and seemingly in bare survival mode.

We worked on, attuned to our environment, pacing ourselves to conserve energy, for the rest of the day was before us. Then, from the trunk of that fine tree there came a quite loud croak! We were nonplussed, we couldn't see how such a noise could be. It came again, it sounded like a frog, but it was coming from the cabbage tree, and trees don't croak! How could there be a frog, in this hot dry piece of land? It croaked some more, there was no doubt, that somehow, there was a frog, right there inside that cabbage tree.

We looked about and took a hint, there was an orchid, a Cymbidium I think, perched in a hollow crotch where a branch had fallen years ago. That orchid is not a true epiphyte because it has roots that go down inside the trunk, and it needed at least some water to survive. But we were near the end of seasonal drought. We wondered, how does this tree support it, and what is that croaking sound about? Now thoroughly absorbed by our curiosity, we downed our tools and looked more closely at the tree. There was a small dead hollow branch; we broke it off and looked inside the tree and saw the roots of that Cymbidium trailing down inside the hollow trunk. We strained our eyes and then we saw the frog, right down there below. They were both immersed in water, clear liquid water, contained inside the tree, and the orchid and the frog had been surviving in it.

I wondered then, how can that be, at the end of such a dry? How did that water get in there; was it from last wet season's rains, or did the tree procure it from its roots? Was that the water used to make the bright new canopy? How did that tree seem to know that rain was coming, already on its way, and that it was safe to grow new leaves? What signal tipped it off, that we were unaware of? Not just that one cabbage gum, but all its cabbage mates?

Whatever it was, the frog was doing well, and the orchid too, inside that cabbage tree. I doubt a botanist could explain it; perhaps we should ask the Aborigines.

A Northern Territory olive python

I'm not afraid of snakes, but there are limits. As long as they go about their business and let me go about mine, that's OK. But I never imagined that they could be managed as well as this bloke managed them.

We were in the Daly Basin in the Northern Territory upon a mapping job, at a time when cattle stations were vast and largely undeveloped. At that time "cattle hunting" would describe Station operations better than true management. The cattle bred up in the wild, and as many as possible were mustered a couple of times a year; some were drafted off for sale, and whatever calves turned up were branded and let loose to breed some more. Things were free and spacious in those days. There had been a motley of occupation before the cattle stations were formally defined, and squatters for whatever reason had settled on the banks of creeks and eked out a living from duffing someone else's cattle, or perhaps a bit of mining. Many of them were fugitives from something or other.

We had been out in the bush for a fortnight and were travelling across country, when we came upon the remnants of an ancient dwelling, now just rusty sheets of iron, lying flat upon the ground. A few decrepit wooden stumps were still in evidence, a scattering of ancient nails, and an old bottle and a horseshoe lay where the hut had stood. There was an old, diseased and white-ant ridden mango tree alongside the hut which we had identified on our aerial photographs, and which was what had aroused our curiosity and attracted us to this spot in the first place.

I had two Toyota four-wheel drives and a team of four good men, all competent bushmen. The ecologist was a man called Ron, he was an experienced old Eurasian and knew a thing or two about the bush that the rest of us did not. As we pulled up he looked around, and when he saw those rusty sheets of iron he gave a knowing nod. We wondered what he sensed, but for the moment we were too immersed in exploration to ask him what had crossed his mind.

It was time for smoko, so we cast around for firewood, lit a fire and boiled the billy, and enjoyed a cup of tea in the shade of the old mango tree. As conversation flagged, one man thought to ask old Ron what it was that he had observed as we arrived at this place. Without a word, he walked across to the remains of the old hut. He lifted up one rusty sheet of iron and exposed a group of snakes, olive pythons, three of them, all very large and tangled up together, at peace and quite content, enjoying the warmth and shelter of their chosen place. Now that was bold!

He knew that they were there, but we had no idea, perhaps he saw their tracks. Needless to say, we were surprised, and immediately went across to take a look. The snakes were stirring now, writhing gently as they untangled and began to extend to their full length. These were very large snakes. We didn't know it then, but the show had only just begun. Ron, with proprietorial pride, declared that he could tame and train them. Of course, we thought that this was just a joke, he was pulling our legs, and as bushmen do, we goaded him on and insisted that this wild claim be put to the test. We thought he would just laugh and back down.

But no. To our further surprise he then proclaimed that it was possible to drive them, that he could guide and steer them, to anywhere he wished. At that we all stood back, and as we watched he reached down into the tangle and took one firmly by the tail. We then stood even further back, for pythons can and do bite, and although they aren't venomous their bite is about as dirty as a goanna's or a horse bite and serious infection is sure to follow. We were immediately concerned that it might turn and try to bite him.

But this man knew a thing or two, there was no problem there, we quickly learned, he knew just how to guide it. He took a backward step, still holding the snake by its tail. His secret was that he didn't push or shoo it, he pulled it back, just a gentle backward pull, and against that tug it struggled. The big snake stretched and strained to be free, it went straight forth, it pulled against the tug upon its tail in order to be shot of and avoid that unwelcome dragging back.

And thus Ron steered that snake, on all his chosen courses. He steered it just by pulling back, he made it go in all directions, by gently pulling back in every opposite one. He sent it just to where he wished, for the next ten minutes. If he was back in Asia he could have walked it home.

You wouldn't try it with a venomous snake, but we were all amazed that he could steer a ten-foot python, at least as heavy as a dog, just by pulling on its tail!

The boar of Nathan River

There are some big pigs in the Australian bush and I've met a few of them, and without exception they are nasty customers, always ready and willing to do you an injury. On this occasion I met a very big boar. It is said that if a big boar gets you down you won't get up again, and I believe it. This one didn't have to get me down, I was already lying down.

We had made a fuel dump on Nathan River Station, close to a large billabong not far from the Limmen Bight River, in what is now the Limmen National Park. I had selected this spot on aerial photographs before we left Darwin, and with the permission of the owner/manager of the station who at that time was a woman, we planned to use this spot as our base for a couple of weeks. I flew there with the helicopter; the others drove the vehicles around through Roper Bar. This was an excellent spot for our working base, with clean ground, good shade, plenty of space to park the helicopter and make our fuel dump and set up our camp.

But the water wasn't as good as we'd thought. It was a large lagoon alright, but it was shallow, and full of water lilies. Maybe that was a seasonal thing because the lilies didn't show up on the aerial photographs, probably because the photos had been flown just after the wet season when the lagoon was full and clean. When we arrived, the water was a bit on the turbid side; we didn't know why at that stage but that didn't really worry us, we were only going to use it for cooking and washing. We found a clear spot along the bank where we could easily take out water for our needs and mount a bush shower, a canvas one with a small Robin engine-driven pump, so we were happy enough.

Well up slope from the lagoon we all chose places for our swags. A swag for a couple of weeks is different from just an overnight one. Here, we selected spots where our beds would be in whatever shade there was for the hottest part of the day, so that they would be relatively cool at night when we went to bed. We set up mosquito nets and light tarpaulin flys to keep such things as bird or flying fox shit or falling leaves off our swags and made places to park our boots and other things. Then we helped the cook to set up his bush kitchen, dragged in some firewood, stowed the scientific gear, tidied up the helipad, and prepared for work next day.

As dusk fell, we had our meal amidst the calling of the dingoes, the settling of the birds and the croaking of the frogs down in the lagoon. It was all quite peaceful, and bonhomie and contentment reigned all around. But unexpectedly, our first night there was disturbed by hordes of feral pigs. They came in droves, and entered in the shallow waters of the lagoon to eat the lily roots, which was why the water was so turbid. We heard the pigs, we were used to them, but at first we couldn't place another sound, a sound like pistol shots. The pigs were plunging their heads down through the shallow water to the bottom mud and rooting around to get the lily roots. As they rose to take a breath, they shook their heads to expel water from their ears, and the flapping of their wet ears made those sounds like pistol shots. Fortunately, we were camped a small distance from the lagoon and the pigs mostly left us alone and came and went to the lagoon regardless of us, so as time went on we began to just ignore them.

But one night, after our day's work was done and all our yarning had subsided, I was lying there inside my swag, eyes half shut and on my way to sleep, when I heard a sound that woke me in an instant. I heard a big boar grunt, right beside my mosquito net. What a shock! This boar must have come to check us out, for that lagoon was his place and we were the usurpers, and not only that, our camp smelled of food. What was I to do? He was right there beside me, I was lying down, there was only a mosquito net between us, and never had a mosquito net seemed so fragile. I remembered the adage, if a big boar gets you down you won't get up again.

Slowly, I loosened my mosquito net on the side away from the pig and reached out underneath my camp stretcher to get my rifle, which was always there in case of need. This was need all right! The pig's hoarse grunting was now more like a squealing roar, mingled with the gnashing of his tusks. He was angry, right there beside me, and I had no choice, it was him or me. Carefully I brought my rifle up, and right through my mosquito net, I fired.

It killed the boar and woke the camp. I gave him a couple more to make sure. And I tell you what, he was a corker! I've never seen so big a boar. As the ringing of the rifle shots died away, I smelled another smell; I turned to check my swag and saw that my mosquito net was smouldering. The point-blank shot had set it alight, so now I had mosquitoes to contend with as well!

Needless to say, next day we all shifted our swags a bit further away from that lagoon.

That bloody spider

Spiders are all very well in their place, but they are not really my thing, especially when they come upon me unexpectedly and at close range. There was one I had an intimate experience with that I will always remember with revulsion.

This time we were way down in the southern part of the Ord River catchment, in remote semi-desert terrain. It was parched, dry, bakingly hot country, and without water a man might not survive a day. In this sort of harsh terrain I had established clear rules of conduct for my team designed to ensure survival, which had to be obeyed, for if things went wrong, if there was no clear strategy, we could be in serious trouble. We made sure that we always knew exactly where we were, the helicopter pilot also, and so did our employers back in Darwin, at least in general terms. If we left the helicopter and proceeded on foot, all of us, pilot included, had to be well apprised of these very definite rules.

We were not always able to land just where we wanted to, so at many landing sites it was necessary to leave the helicopter and walk off into the scrub to pre-determined sites marked on our aerial photographs, which we would then describe and record for the purposes of our work. Afterwards we would re-locate the chopper, often on a reverse compass course, then fly on to the next spot. One of the strategies we employed was to plan our investigation sites more or less in a line between two landing sites, land at the first one, then send the chopper on to the second landing spot at the other end of the survey line. We would then walk towards the distant place where the helicopter had landed, doing our survey work along the way. This sounds easy enough, but once out of sight of the helicopter, finding it again in all that trackless country can be like finding a needle in a haystack, and it is very easy indeed to become lost.

It was all planned. We landed, disembarked, maintaining full revs on the rotors, and the pilot took off again immediately. At the distant site he was to land straight down and slowly, so that I could take a compass bearing on the chopper as a real measurement, for the plan drawn on the aerial photographs was subject to distortion and therefore significant error. I had estimated that it would take two and a half hours for us to complete the traverse and arrive at the second landing site with the helicopter. There was a pre-arranged fail-safe procedure with the pilot. If we were late, he was to sound the starter, so that if we were mis-located but nearby we would hear the noise and home in on it. Fifteen minutes later he was to start the turbine, which produced a much louder noise, and lift up vertically into the air so that we could re-establish a compass course and walk towards it. Thirty minutes later, if we still hadn't returned, he was to take off and do an airborne search to find and save us.

I had a team of three disciplined scientists with me, plus of course the helicopter pilot. My ground staff and a helicopter engineer were back at our base camp, close to Inverway Station. We had landed on quite hostile ground, hot and uncompromisingly dry. The shrubby growth was just tall enough to block our view ahead, and I had to find a small clearing to take my compass bearing on the helicopter as it landed. With the chopper gone it was very still and quiet, except for a faint throbbing in the ears as the sun bore down, and a strong sense of isolation. We checked our gear, re-affirmed the compass course and wrote it down, and with me in front, set off on foot towards the first of our inspection sites.

I had my compass, maps and aerial photographs all to hand. The men behind me, bushmen all, strong and very hardy, were all psyched up for what might lie before us.

One man carried my rifle, for without it we could be at the mercy of any shorthorn bulls we met, another had our water. Tracking to my compass course we walked across the country. I held my line, I watched my course, avoiding bits of scrub, focusing entirely on the task at hand. My men were silent, taking in the plan. Then something that I didn't plan and hadn't even dreamed about occurred. All at once I realized that I'd walked into a spider's web, and I had the spider on me, and in an instant, I completely lost the plot.

It was a St. Andrews Cross type of spider. I saw it briefly from the corner of my eye, but it was slow to register on my awareness through the focus of my work, and I walked right into it. It was a strong and yellow web, and very sticky. I had it plastered on my chest from chin to waist, and bits of it were on my hands and arms. It just engulfed me, unawares. And the occupant of the web was there upon my chest, scrabbling fast, thinking every moment was its last, and so was I. I could feel its frantic movement, it tried to run upwards, towards my neck, but its own web had it trapped.

There was a time of comprehension, it didn't last so long, I would guess about a millisecond, and then my focus changed; revulsion and self-survival instincts all hit home, and my casual observation turned instantly to horror. This energetic spider was a monster, so big it would fit quite neatly into my quart pot.

Then in immediate panic mode I threw away, I didn't care, the compass, photos, all my gear, straight across the scrub, and I tore in frenzy at my breast to get that spider off my chest. I ran, and cursed, and kicked up dust, whilst struggling hard to get it off. Yellow web was everywhere, the spider still aboard. And my good team, perceiving what they'd seen, were filled with instant mirth. Their discipline and training all turned to naught, and they laughed so hard that they could hardly stand. No-one shared my plight, none came up to help me. One put down his things and collapsed to laugh upon the ground.

Eventually, I shed the beast and the last scraps of the web, and thus divested, regained my former composure. My good men recovered all my things, and thus we all came back to earth. I'm sure that they had seen it coming and were waiting with amusement for my reaction. It was harmless, all agreed, but I will always loathe that spider.

Anopheles Creek

In all my life I've never known mosquitoes quite like this. They're never welcome, and in some places they can be thick, but this place was by far the worst of all.

I've often thought about it, and asked myself how careless one can be, but then again, I guess there are some things one doesn't know about until afterwards. It cannot be escaped though that in my preparations I had made a sad mistake. Back at the office I had been planning a base camp for a team of men, using maps and aerial photographs, to select a place in the bush for them (and me) to live in for a month. I had committed us all to camping in that particular spot, without ever having been there or sent a man to check it out. That turned out to be a big mistake.

This was in the Northern Territory, near the Port Keats Aboriginal Settlement, now known as Wadeye. It was quite near the access road, and easy to get to with four-wheel drive vehicles. It was flat, open alluvial plains country with good shade trees, and there was an ideal place beside the camp site to park the helicopter and locate a fuel dump. Best of all, there was a permanent creek with a beautiful tree-lined waterhole that looked quite clear and deep from the aerial photographs, which was important as we would need drinking and process water and had to bathe regularly. It really seemed ideal, I'd checked it out quite thoroughly, I thought, it appeared to be a perfect spot to base our operations from, and the creek would keep the ground staff happy whilst the airborne crew were away during the day. I'd thought of crocodiles, feral pigs, snakes and rats. I knew the ground was firm, and that the helipad was ideal. I didn't know it then, but there was one thing I had overlooked, something I hadn't even thought of, I should have guessed, it was a gift, the creek was clearly marked on the topographic maps, its name was plain, it was called Anopheles Creek.

From Darwin, I sent the ground staff off to pitch the camp, with a truckload of drums of helicopter fuel. When I had radio confirmation that the camp was all set up, I flew from Darwin to Port Keats in a light plane to join them, and the team picked me up from the airstrip and took me to the camp. The timing was a bit tight because the helicopter was coming in that evening. The first thing I noticed was that in the fuel dump the drums were all standing neatly on their ends. This was a definite no-no, the pilot would not use the fuel because the daily expansion and contraction of the drums might cause any accumulated water to be sucked in through the seals and contaminate the fuel, so I immediately ordered all those drums to be pushed over onto their sides. The rest of the camp seemed fine, the tents were up, there was a large shady tarpaulin for general use, and plenty of good places for our swags. My men had done well.

But there was something desolate about this camp. All the men seemed strangely quiet, not at all their usual exuberant selves. They seemed pre-occupied, and were slapping at their arms and legs in a desultory sort of way. No-one said anything to me, so I placed my survey gear beneath the tarp, selected a nice shady tree and unrolled my swag beside it. Why I didn't notice it before I do not know, but suddenly it hit me, those men already knew something that I was just finding out. The whole bloody place was infested with mosquitoes! Infested! It was alive with them! The place was ruled by insects; mosquitoes, it seemed, were there in strength. With sinking heart, I recalled the name, Anopheles Creek.

As dusk came on and the chopper hove in sight, the full import of this plague dawned upon me. We would have to endure a month of this, because there was no way we could re-load those fuel drums now that they had been dropped off.

Of all the insect pests that plague us I used to think that the dawn to dark bushflies were the worst, but I was wrong, now I know better, the mosquitoes win hands down. I've experienced them in New Guinea, and I'm told they're bad in the Tundra, but I couldn't imagine anything worse than what befell us here.

No man could know how many mossies, each one bigger than the last, were there on that occasion, it was beyond all comprehension. I tell you, they were manifold, and present in their millions. They came in droves, they savaged us, each foray more voracious than the last. We killed them in their thousands, but more came in to fill the gaps, they were queuing up to bite us. At dusk, a veritable cloud of them would rise from near the creek and move ominously towards us, engulfing us, a never-ending constant horde of infuriating insects, standing on their heads to stab us, biting, stinging, and chomping, amidst a constant penetrating whine. What was worse, they didn't quit at daybreak, they left battalions with us in the tents to bite and chew at every chance, they'd just sneak up on us and chomp. I knew full well the Aussie outback wave, that casual hand across the face to chase the flies away, but we invented something else, a full-blown energetic dance, a frantic sort of bushman's slapstick theatre.

We burnt mosquito coils, we burned cow dung, we wore full clothes, we even put on boiler suits. We spread repellent, we fought them off with fly swats, but in spite of smoke and clothes and all our curses, they stayed. There was no end to them. Considerable quantities of verbal abuse were constantly applied, but to no avail. I think they had a scheme, a sort of roster. Whilst one horde attacked, intent and fierce, a spare million-odd would rest, perched inside the tents awaiting further chompings, until the first wave was repelled, then they would enter into the fray and re-invigorate their team.

Even when we went to bed inside mosquito nets we had to seek and kill the ones that got inside with us before we could lie down and rest. Though cheated of their blood those pests stayed on guard outside, preventing all the sleep they could with an incessant, droning moan, punctuated at intervals by a muffled curse, expletives, or a clearly aimed directive to go to hell and stay there, when a careless sleeper laid his arm against his net.

Each day at sunrise the field team went off inside the chopper, relieved at last for the duration of the day, but the poor ground staff were persecuted almost past their ability to cope. In late afternoon when we returned, they emerged from cover looking haggard, worn and spent, covered in itchy spots as though a pox had come upon them, which it had, yet then they had to start again and endure another night. And every evening, as we wrote our work into the daily survey book, there came again vast clouds of mossies, and so we soldiered on, midst constant slaps and curses. By the end of that job we were intent that all mosquitoes should most definitely be shot.

Curiously, no-one had told me, not the Port Keats staff when I requested permission to camp there, and not my own staff when we spoke on the radio after they had established the camp. Maybe they thought that I already knew about it and had some scheme to combat the little buggers. Perhaps no-one had ever been there at night!

We endured that camp until the end, whilst carrying out that job. We never solved the problem; the mosquitoes had the numbers. But I'll tell you this, when I take out and shake that daily survey book, preserved mosquitoes fall out from in between the pages; the mossies of that camp come floating out, a record of Anopheles Creek.

Our camp upon the Ord

When we came in to Kununurra from our work in the bush we used to camp beside the Ord River, below the Lake Kununurra diversion dam. We usually arrived in Kununurra in the late afternoon and spent some time at the pub having a meal and several welcome beers. Then we would go down to the Ord to our special place to camp. There was a track on the left bank just across the weir that led down to the water. It was a popular spot, frequented by the tourists, because it was the only place they could get to that was near the water, but it was a dirty place, full of flies and rubbish. We were used to the clean and peaceful bush and had no wish to camp with those tourists, and their flies and rubbish.

We had been to this area before, in daylight, because we often finished up in Kununurra and needed a place to camp, so we had reconnoitred to find a suitable spot. We had found the ideal place. It was a lovely spot, almost level, on a warm and grassy bank of the lower Ord not far below the diversion dam, where we had plenty of room to park three vehicles and spread out our swags, and there was always plenty of driftwood for the fire. But we could only get there by driving down actually in the river, vehicles partly submerged, for eighty metres or so until we reached our grassy low levee.

In low range, we would enter into the river at this tourist spot and drive downstream in the shallows close beside the riverbank to our clean and peaceful spot, climb out of the river and up onto this low grassy bank, and have it to ourselves. No tourist would be game to follow us because it involved driving in the water with the crocodiles, and a good, waterproofed four-wheel drive vehicle, a knowledge of the river and of these saurians, and experienced bush drivers who knew what they were doing were essential. So, no tourists, and none of their flies and rubbish!

Now, we all have bosses, and some are more approachable than others. Ours was a good one, he had to be, because we were working in the bush, and bullshit doesn't cut when you're near the nitty gritty. We knew this guy well, and his failings, but even so we weren't able to predict all that he might do. This time he sprung a new one on us. He was with us one night in Kununurra; he had flown down to attend a meeting in the town on the future of the Ord Irrigation Scheme, and afterwards, by arrangement, he met up with us to spend the night. We already had his swag along with ours in the back of one of our vehicles. We met in town and spent time at the pub, discussing the outcome of his meeting and the progress of our work in the bush. It was a pleasant time and I guess we spent rather longer at the pub than we should have. Then, feeling quite exuberant, we went down to the river and drove down in the shallows to our grassy camping place. We set up camp and went to bed, and all seemed well.

But halfway through the night our boss woke up. He seemed a bit dis-orientated, and no wonder, straight from Darwin to the dark and steamy banks of the Ord River, and all that beer. He mumbled that he had just remembered something, he had an appointment with a colleague back in town. He rose and dressed and started one of our Toyotas, intent on returning to the town and attending his "meeting". But he forgot that to get to the camping place we were in, we had driven very carefully down the water's edge in the shallows, close against the riverbank, and he drove instead directly into the Ord and straight towards the other side. The other side! The Ord! Not possible, this was a big river. We were half asleep, but now we very quickly came awake – there was no way he could drive across that river, it was the middle of the night, the water was very deep, it was infested with crocodiles, and he was not quite himself.

When the water rose halfway up the cab and was pouring in upon him, the engine steaming, he hit a rock and stalled, and seemed to come to his senses and gave up his attempt. We were horrified, and felt responsible, our boss was in dire trouble. No amount of shouting had any effect, he probably couldn't hear us above the noise of the engine and the river. However, he wasn't far away from the bank, so notwithstanding the crocodiles we leaped into the river and fished him out. Our vehicle was by now fully dunked, and unable to move under its own power. We guddled around in waist deep water, with those crocodiles surely lurking somewhere about, attached a cable to the tow bar, started up another vehicle and pulled our very wet Toyota out.

And we told our boss, firmly, because we knew, look mate, there are no appointments late at night in Kununurra!

The cane toad scourge

One sees photographs of these beasts and we saw them often in the wild, and some of them are remarkably large. They are a pest, and a poisonous one, and with that sort of publicity they always seem to invoke feelings of revulsion, and have been lampooned, beaten up, squashed and generally maltreated. There was a time in my camp when these feelings came to the fore and a concerted attack was mounted against them.

We were camped on Calvert Hills Station during a Gulf country survey job. We'd picked an excellent campsite, with good water, shade of sorts, plenty of room for the cook's tent, our office caravan and all our swags, and a perfect place to accommodate the helicopter and a fuel dump. We even had a bush shower rigged up down beside the creek. This was to be a three-week field job, so as well as the scientific crew of four we had a camp cook and a couple of ground staff, two four-wheel drives, and an aircraft engineer to service and maintain the helicopter. We were very well set up.

There were other teams about as well, mineral exploration teams with a geologist and some roughnecks in bush camps close to the homestead, or at one of their out-stations. There were also mustering crews with groups of ringers or jackaroos at cattle camps scattered around the country, as it was annual mustering time. The exploration teams had helicopters, one of the mustering camps did too, although they were all smaller craft than ours, and the ringers and the roughnecks had motorbikes and four-wheel drives. So the country was fairly busy, for a piece of outback bush.

At that time, the cane toad scourge was well and truly on us. These toads had walked up from Queensland over a number of wet seasons, and we were right on the frontal wave of them as they advanced. They were there in droves, hiding under rocks and logs by day but scuttling around the camp at night, so thickly that their tracks obliterated all our day-time footprints. Some of them were large enough to half fill a bucket, they must have weighed a kilogram or more. After work, when the roughnecks were sitting down to rest with a beer or several, they used the toads as a diversion from the continual heat and flies of the bush. They said that they were training them; they had toads in various situations, tied to the legs of chairs, hanging from branches of trees and otherwise being tormented.

According to regulations, one day each week our pilot had to have a rest, and that was supposed to apply to the mineral exploration and mustering pilots too. Sunday was the best day, and on that day all the helicopters stayed on their pads and the crews stayed in their camps. In our camp, we settled down to do our washing, read, and write up notes. The ringers and the roughnecks amused themselves as best they could in their respective camps.

These bush people habitually talked between their camps, especially the helicopter pilots with their radios, and we were all pretty much aware of what the other groups were doing. There was talk of a get-together on one Sunday. We had the best location, the largest camp, and there was no doubt that we had the best facilities; and we had that rare luxury in the bush, a helicopter engineer. So, on one Sunday afternoon, all of them came to our camp for a visit.

The pilots came in first, soon after lunch. As well as ours there were three visiting helicopters around the edges of our landing pad, and a few extra four-wheel drives and a motorbike or two were parked alongside ours, and there was an influx of additional men around the camp. There was quite a lot of beer about and many of the visitors and our own crew had already had a bit to drink. Like most of these affairs there was no food on offer, nobody wanted it anyway. As the day wore on and several beers had been consumed everyone was feeling relaxed; and ever inventive, the ringers, roughnecks and the pilots formed a plan.

It wasn't clear at first what they were intending to do, but they set about making what they called a "cane toad launcher" out of several steel soft-drink cans. The tops and bottoms of the cans were removed and the cans were bound in line, secured with fibreglass-reinforced sticky tape, to form a kind of tube, or "barrel" as it turned out to be. The bottom can had only the normal rip-top piece removed, then they punched just a small hole in the lower edge of this can, and bound it on below the others. The small hole was to inject the methylated spirits primer, or as it turned out, the explosive. This was their cane toad launcher; it was very like a small military mortar.

Then they rushed around and caught some toads, of a size to suit the launcher. They stuffed one down inside the barrel, and as indignant toads do, he puffed his body out, and nicely filled the breech. Then they poured some methylated spirits into the priming hole and struck a match and fired it. With a bang, the toad was off and flying, for more than thirty metres! Then those enterprising pilots came up with an improvement to the game.

One of them scuttled round and found a piece of wood shaped something like a cricket bat, and like a classy cricketer he went out and hit them back. The launcher was primed and fired again and again. The batsman "declared" (in local terms) and was replaced, after failing to pay attention and being bombed by a splayed-out toad. The batsmen had to run around a bit because the toads had to be hit on the full, as once one hit the ground it didn't bounce. There was close to pandemonium, toad fragments were flying in all directions, and any excuse was called upon to pronounce the batsman "out". But I had to stop it in the end, when the ringers lost control of the propellant and nearly set the cookhouse tent alight.

But all agreed, although it did seem wild, it was a "conservation" game, for cane toads were a pest. I guess the RSPCA would have had a few words to say about it though. And wobbly, but in control, those bush pilots flew back home. I know they all returned home safely, but crikey, what a Sunday!

That helicopter pilot

In my experience, the best helicopter pilots were those who had returned from the Vietnam war. But ex-Vietnam pilots weren't quite normal, they didn't fly according to the generally accepted commercial pilot's procedure. I navigate helicopters and have flown with all sorts of pilots in all sorts of conditions, and I knew these ex-war types. They had been used to rapid take offs and landings to avoid enemy fire and had developed some interesting strategies, and out of habit and choice they flew their craft for all that it could safely do, regardless of the comfort of its occupants. They were skilled pilots, and I found their style of flying stimulating and efficient, and I was well used to their ways of going and their antics.

As usual on these jobs I was supposed to accommodate senior staff from Darwin on some of the flights so that they could see something of the country, and I was also supposed to train new recruits, so it was quite common to have neophytes in the rear seat of the helicopter. These pilots were unconcerned about bad weather. One day there were quite high winds, and we had no option but to progress sideways. The pilot could do nothing about it, the wind was blowing the tail around so that we could only go crabwise. There was no point in looking out of the front windscreen because that showed me the landscape that was actually off to the left, so I was forced to navigate through the pilot's side window. But undeterred, this bloke saw no problem. He just laughed. Never mind the orientation, he said, we're still on track, what are you worried about? But it was rough going, and I'm sure my rear seat passengers were not too comfortable.

Ordinary domestic helicopter pilots take off gradually as a small plane does, fly in nice straight lines, and coming down they take their time. They haul the helicopter back, pointing straight ahead, tail low, and gradually slow it down, then they level out and make a gentle graceful landing. But not these ex-Vietnam types. On this survey job we had an ex-Vietnam pilot, and landing was his special talent. If there was one thing he could do, and do well, it was to land a helicopter in a hurry. There were two parts to his technique, and he used them both habitually. One day, when we were searching for a particular landing site, I as navigator said, "There, in that clearing just below, is where I want to land", and so the pilot put in train his rapid landing sequence, part one. At cruising speed, he pulled the stick and put the chopper straight up to the sky. It quickly stalled, our airspeed down to zero. Then he changed the tail rotor pitch by 180 degrees, the machine spun around instantly through half a circle, and from a view of clear blue sky we were suddenly looking straight down at the land. At breakneck speed, he shot us straight towards the ground, it seemed as though we'd crash. He quashed the turbine, auto rotated, the altimeter unwinding fast, and we descended at what seemed to be a good part of the speed of sound. But I knew what was coming next. He had it full in hand, he pulled out at the last, and shot along above the ground. He brought back power, his airspeed still quite fast, and cruised towards our landing site.

Then came his rapid landing sequence, part two. He threw the craft completely on its side and used the blades, and turbine power, to quickly slow it down, then he swung it back upright and dropped us, faultless, right upon that piece of ground. At no time did we feel anything other than normal direct G forces, we never even swayed in our seats, it was perfect execution. But fast! I reckon that the landing, from my initial request, all up, took about twenty seconds.

But he'd landed in a clearing with tall trees all around, and after we had done our work I could see no way that we could exit, all together in one load. The machine was not capable of vertical take-off with this load aboard, and I envisaged ferrying us out in two or more hops. Then we discovered that take-offs were his second special talent. No problem, he said, get in. He started up the turbine and whacked around the clearing in tiny circles until we hit translational speed, then lifted up above the trees.

This ex-war pilot, like others of his kind, gave no concession to the un-initiated. I was used to these performances, I had them every day, but some were not, as I deduced whilst on that flight. For I have never seen, upon the bar behind my seat, a neater row of tight white knuckles. But I contend that for safety and competence, those wartime pilots were the best. But hell, ex Vietnam war pilots!

Bird eating spiders

It is interesting that something as small and inconspicuous as a spider can cause grown men to panic. It was probably understandable in this case because there were several spiders, and they weren't small. But my field crew's reaction to these ones was somewhat extreme.

We were well equipped, efficient, and all working hard and happily. We were out on the Weaber Plain, part of the broader Ord River plains in the Northern Territory, mapping land for irrigation. We were investigating different patterns that showed on aerial photographs, and were slogging across the plains on various compass courses doing our soil assessment work as we went. There was another team out there as well, compiling topographic data. They had theodolites and were producing a detailed map of the level of the land, for irrigation canal and access-road layout. They also had a grader and were using it to prepare a grid of lines scraped clean for follow-up seismic survey work.

It was as hot as hell. The land was rough, because the whole soil surface was gilgaied or "melon-holed" and full of shrinkage cracks. It was covered in dry tussocks of grass and prickly Acacia shrubs (Acacia bidwillii) and even walking was difficult. In places it was so rough that it would be easy to twist an ankle, and any step was peril. And so we chose to camp that night on one of the graded seismic survey lines that our colleagues had prepared.

We set up camp. We parked the vehicles on the line, gathered wood, laid a fire, and set out our swags in preparation for the night. We helped our designated cook prepare our dinner, and we ate, drank a billy of tea and relaxed at evening peace.

Then one good man, an observant chap, said "what are all those holes about?" We looked; there were quite a number of them, strangely, we hadn't noticed them before. They were quite large circular holes about 40-50 millimetres across, the openings of tunnels down into the ground, scattered far and wide along the graded line. It seemed they had been revealed by the grader's cut, they must have been there all along, but were inconspicuous in that rough terrain until the land was cleared of vegetation and levelled by the grader. A good question; what were they? What made them? Did anything live in them? So we thought we would carry out a test, and discover whether they were occupied, and if so, by what.

We made a liquid slurry, petrol mixed with water, and poured it into one of the holes. We waited, but nothing happened. We tried another hole. No response. We tried several more holes, but there was no sign of rejoinder. We began to think that the holes were uninhabited. Then, to get rid of it, we poured our slurry down a lot more holes, yet none came up to answer, and we concluded that the holes were empty, possibly relics of a wet season population of something or other, mice perhaps. And so we all sat down again to carry on our banter.

The sun was going down and light was fading, when all at once there was a vision. Right in front of us, from one big hole, the first one we had treated, there unfolded one great spider. He came out slowly, masked in petrol, and then he opened out, a huge brown hairy spider, and I tell you mate it seemed to us he would have spanned a generous dinner plate.

Well I've been out bush for quite a while but never have I seen four sound and solid bushmen go straight up on the vehicles. They had twigged, that this was one, but there was petrol down so many holes, any one or all of which might harbour spiders, and at any moment more of them might suddenly appear, and they might not be too pleased. And when at last those men did come down, they paused atop the trucks and carefully looked around, before descending to the ground. We stoked the fire and kept our torches handy, our banter ceased, replaced by constant furtive looks in all directions. And so that night we slept in somewhat of a lather, and I'll tell you what, we kept our mosquito nets very tightly around us. Next morning there were seven dead such spiders, and we shook and packed our gear and vanished fast, never to camp again on a graded seismic survey line.

We found somewhat later that they were northern bird eating spiders.

The ringers' quarters on Mainoru

Out in the field my team would say of me when walking through the bush that because I was the fittest I should lead, and along with that take all the responsibility, which meant of course taking all the blame as well. I'd been doing all that anyway because I was the team leader. It had been a long walk, I know, but my men were strong and resilient and were never more than a hundred metres or so behind me, which isn't very much in the bush. However, all this exertion took its toll and when we returned to camp in the evening we were always hot and sweaty and looking forward to a bath.

It was a job I'd been contracted to do and had been planning for quite some time, checking out the land and what sort of uses it might be capable of. We had a Squirrel helicopter, a very good machine for us, and Mainoru Station had welcomed us. We were lucky to be there and were well accommodated in the ringers' quarters. We had single rooms, real beds and even a decent cook, not to mention a plentiful supply of beef. And Mainoru had lots of water. But due to that there was one clear and terrible disadvantage, because they used some of that water to maintain their lawns.

Lawns grow pretty fast in Mainoru, and given the over-riding dryness all around, that green grass attracted some attention. The cattle were too frightened, or dumb maybe, to come in and partake, but with the gumption of the bush the buffalo had cottoned on. With due regard for their own safety they waited until the dusk, and shortly afterwards some of them would venture in, the same ones every time, and feast upon that lawn. They were large and handy beasts, full of courage, very territorial, and at night were willing to indulge in anything at all. After dark, that was their lawn.

Then there were the cattle dogs, several of them, and like the rest of their breed they were also willing to indulge in any lark that came along. These were lean and hardened dogs toughened by their work, and also territorial. They had a sort of truce with the buffalo and would chastise them only sometimes, just for sport as it were, and would most likely come off second best. Then there were us, me and my team. I know we'd been feasting on "sugarbag" honey that we sometimes found in the bush, but surely that could be no excuse for the regular evening lunacy that followed.

There we were, housed in the ringers' quarters. The problem was that the ablution block was over there, across the lawn, and to get to it we had to cross that lawn. Because we worked every daylight hour we had to shower after dark, by which time those buffalo had already come in to feed upon the lawns. And then there was their precarious truce with the cattle dogs. These were bush buffalo and had scant regard for dogs, to these beasts, dogs were just things to be kicked and tossed around.

What a scene. We had to wash because we were so sweaty and grimy, but the shower block was across the lawn. It became our evening's entertainment, with all of us as the performers. We'd take off all our clothes, wrap a towel around us, and rush one by one as fast and spritely as we could, dodging first the buffalo and then the dogs, for if the dogs got offside with the buffalo they'd come for us, or otherwise the buffalo would be onto us. That was fair enough on the way out when we were dirty because we could run and dodge regardless, but getting back again was a problem, because by then the buffs had got us sussed and the cattle dogs knew where we were and had lain in wait for us, and having just washed, we wanted to keep ourselves clean.

There were lots of cunning strategies devised, the best of which was two men at a time, but then the buffs would get one and the cattle dogs the other. It was better than TV. First the shouts of bravado as one man started out to come back home, followed by his squeals of terror as he pranced around the buffalo, and then his desperate pleas to the cattle dogs to lay off. These were naked men, and they had a lot to lose.

It was all go on the lawns at night in Mainoru. I did enjoy that job!

Contretemps with a snake

Snakes have always had significance for me. When I was a young fellow, I could always sense a snake, I think I still can. I used to know that one was there, at least the brown ones. I could sort of "feel" them, and sure enough, one would be there. But it never used to work with pythons; they were different, they had to be visual. I had to actually see them.

My issue at this time was with a python, and he was a big one. Mostly he was quite OK, a guest in our ceiling as a rat and possum catcher, and quite friendly really. He is still there, and I see quite a lot of him, he comes out and basks on the roof at times. But lately he has become a bit of a pest because he has started to come inside the house, almost always at night. At first, I thought he entered through the cat/dog door, probably for the warmth, but if he did he was always gone again by morning. The dog treats him as normal and so doesn't bother to raise an alarm. But this had gotten to be somewhat disconcerting.

My first introduction to him was when I opened the sliding door from our living room to our garage and was faced with a broad, inquisitive-looking head, about 30 centimetres off the floor. He was an unexpected visitor, quite a nice-looking guy, but it was a bit alarming to meet him there, already inside the house. I think he wanted to come further in, because we had the fire going and it was warm inside, but guests usually knock on the door or otherwise announce their intentions. Then I noticed that he had a long body draped behind him, and I began to see that he was a snake. He was just getting down off my wife's computer table. He was a very big snake, a heavy one, a mature diamond python. That was my first close-up meeting with him. Anyway, I took him by his tail out into the garden and let him go, so that he could easily climb into a tree and security. What he did, though, was cross the back lawn and climb back into his roof.

But things went from bad to worse. He kept on coming back. They are like possums, very territorial, they keep on returning to their place. At first, I didn't mind; we've already got a dog, a cat and chooks, not to mention stuff out there in the pond and amongst the vegetables, but this python was beginning to take liberties.

I always liked to have an open house such that wind can flow through as it blows, so the window in the main toilet is always open, just 20 centimetres or so of aperture, along with all the other doors and windows of the house, except for the security screens. One night I went into the toilet and was almost sure I saw that python looking in. I closed the window, feeling a little uneasy. I didn't want him in our bedroom!

But the next night I was quite certain of it, he had his head almost inside the window, same guy. I think he was coming down from his attic onto the top of the electric hot water tank just outside and was stretching out into the toilet. That had to be stopped, I thought, his place was outside. I should have acted then, but I left it one day too late. He came inside.

One does get up at night to go to the toilet or generally enjoy the moonlight, but it is a little unsettling to find yourself treading upon and then tripping over a very large python, not to mention the unknown intent of either of you, something that neither the python nor the human are ready to convey to each other, least of all at that particular time. In that kind of transaction there is no formal agenda, it is a fairly primal and immediate thing. Then there is this unseemly melee, mostly conducted on the floor, with fearful grunts and weird exclamations intermixed with squeals of real terror, which goes on a bit. There is not a lot of good in it. This sort of thing tends to disrupt one's sleep, not to mention that of others around you. Wrestling with pythons in a dark house at night is best left alone. It is an interesting experience, but once is sufficient, and it is not to be recommended to others.

I guess it will be on-going, but you can get enough of pythons.

The road to Jim-Jim Falls

I belonged to the Darwin Land Rover Owners' Club. At intervals, such as at Easter, we used to organize trips out to some lovely but hard to get to place in the bush. Easter was a good time because the wet season was over, but the streams were still running well, and access was becoming possible for well set up four-wheel drive vehicles. This time we planned to try to get to Jim-Jim Falls, a fabled but known to be spectacular waterfall, coming off the Arnhem Land escarpment. This was before the Kakadu National Park was in place. I was well versed in cross-country navigation as I did a lot of it as part of my work, and I had access to aerial photographs, so I was nominated to be expedition leader.

Back in Darwin one weekend I assembled the air photos and topographic maps and looked for the best course to take. I knew of a good starting point already, as I had investigated it on a previous trip out that way. With my stereoscope, I plotted a course that avoided wet, steep or otherwise untrafficable areas and marked a preferred course on the photos. Then, with my vehicle packed, I was ready to roll.

We met as planned in the early morning at the Club headquarters. We had four Land Rovers including my own, and a motley lot of people. There weren't any women, which was probably fortuitous as things turned out. The men were all experienced bush drivers, wide-ranging in personality, but all of them were fully enthusiastic and raring to go. We set off in convoy eastwards towards Arnhem Land, along the road to Cahills Crossing on the East Alligator River and Oenpelli. Jabiru didn't exist at that time. We reached the point where we were to begin our traverse and it was time for smoko, a can of beer for most, and to sort out the protocol and order of progression. Spirits were running high.

We left the road, obliterating our initial tracks as well as we could to discourage any curious adventurers who might want to follow us. I had a companion in my vehicle, but he wasn't used to navigating by a path drawn on aerial photographs. This became a problem because I had to drive, and that alone took most of my concentration, but I looked over his shoulder when I could. All went well at first. Then, to my concern, we came across a swamp, which was definitely not on my proposed track. It was a small swamp and there was a way around it, so we went that way. I realized that we could no longer travel in the secure way I had planned, so I used dead reckoning, and drove in a more or less straight line towards where I knew we would find the falls. It was not that difficult, and I began to recognize features that I remembered from my air photo interpretation. By common contrivance there were several beer pauses along the way. The last bit was up a short but quite steep incline, and I advised all drivers on our radios to use low range and keep going straight up. At the top, we could see the gorge below the falls, and such was the jubilation that it was necessary to have another beer stop.

The wetlands below the gorge were fantastic, totally pristine, with crystal clear water running over clean sandy beds, huge paperbark trees (Melaleuca leucadendra) and dappled, sparkling sunlight filtering down through their canopy. There were lots of lizards, insects, completely unafraid little fishes in the water, and everywhere, along with the trickling sound of calm running water, were the songs of myriads of beautiful, colourful birds. It was paradise. We made camp, and predictably, the devotees amongst us had more beer. We had a barbeque that night. Barbeques in the suburbs aren't what they used to be. None of those flash gas-powered things for us, we had an old plough disk and a steel plate to light a fire under, but in keeping with our loyalties, we used what was traditional for us, the grille off one of the Land Rovers.

Early next morning we tidied up the camp and collected our cameras and other gear and began the walk in. Then we could see the falls! They were truly spectacular, running freely and in great abundance, in a huge vertical drop. There was a large, long lagoon to travel beside and we chose the southern bank, with the towering cliffs of the escarpment above us on both sides of the gorge. The forest beside us consisted of only one tree species, Allosyncarpia ternata, an ancient relic of the rain forests of long ago, now retreated to isolated sheltered pockets. Before long we struck a mist, and then the spray, and had to enclose our cameras in plastic bags. The spray soon drenched us, but it was a hot day and we reveled in it. At the base of the falls there was a deep, round, turbulent pool, agitated by the impact of cascading tons of water, and we came to a speechless, astounded halt. It was so spectacular, and the crashing roar of water so deafening; it was absolutely, utterly salutary. And each man made a silent obeisance out of sheer respect, and vowed never to do anything bad in all of his life ever again.

Back in camp we found that we were nearly out of meat, so a couple of enterprising and still fairly sober guys went out and shot a nice young buffalo. Buffs have amazingly thick hides but the meat of a young one is better than beef, and leaner. As the day wore on and more beer was consumed (our ration was a dozen cans per man per day), one fellow sang a song, terribly, another did a soft shoe shuffle (as he remembered it) on the bonnet of his Land Rover, and we all told wild fantastic yarns.

But we had to return to Darwin. That was easy, we just followed our tracks back to the road and headed home. Later, after uranium was discovered there, the Kakadu National Park was established, and the township of Jabiru was built. A proper road was constructed into Jim-Jim Falls, which followed more or less along the track we had forged. So, despite our shenanigans, we did have some small claim to fame!

Bonus: How to light a fire in the bush

Even without matches!

Introduction

A campfire is essential in the bush, and it is very easy to light one if you know how. After starting the fire, it can then be built up depending on what you want to do with it. Two types of fire are described below, a quick one just to boil the billy, and a longer lasting, hotter one for cooking an evening meal. Signal fires are also mentioned.

Collecting the materials

It is a useful start to find a place where a good supply of fuel is clearly available. There are preferred species of tree for firewood wherever you go, such as ironwood in northern Australia or yellow box in the south, but the fallen branches of most eucalyptus trees will burn well if they are dry. Some species of tree do not burn well, for example paperbark; this wood also emits a foul odour when burning. Most types of conifer, especially Pinus, Casuarina and Calytris species produce small detonations and showers of sparks when burning which can make the fire hazardous.

To begin with, collect some tinder. Dry grass or leaf litter is the best initial tinder. Spinifex is excellent, as are dry gum tree leaves. Kindling comes next; the best is thin dry twigs that have fallen from gum trees, but any thin dry twigs will do. Then make piles of small sticks, bigger ones, and then larger more solid pieces. Bits of bark are useful if they are dry. Then collect the main firewood, of sequentially larger sizes, more categories of size if there is no breeze or if the wood is not really dry. Longer lengths can often be broken into pieces by whacking them against a log or stump. If the fire is to be long-lasting it may even be built right against a log or stump. This collection of fuel should be done as soon as the camp has been established, to avoid having to forage around later on, possibly in the dark, for additional wood.

If the wood is damp

At some places there may be both damp wood and dry wood, and it may seem difficult to tell the difference. "Dry" means dry inside; a film of external wetness due to recent rain is not a problem. To ensure internal dryness collect all materials from above the ground surface, either from standing timber, or wood supported so that it is not in contact with the soil. Material that has been lying in direct contact with the soil surface or under surface litter may be moist right inside the wood and will not burn well, if at all. Even if moisture is not visible, a good test is that moist wood usually feels cooler to the hands than dry wood, due to evaporation of the moisture within it.

In wet conditions, even if it is raining at the time, dry kindling can always be found still attached to the smaller trees, including living trees. Almost every small tree or shrub has dead twigs still attached to its branches, and if these are snapped off they will burn as well as, or better than, dry wood because they still retain some volatiles.

It is most important that the initial tinder and kindling are dry. Moist tinder and kindling can be dried by holding them in the exhaust of your vehicle for a while, but be careful not to inhale the exhaust fumes. Once the fire is going it will produce enough heat to dry out subsequent layers of fuel by itself, provided that these are only superficially moist.

Constructing the fire

Select a spot with an adequate cleared area around the fire. In very windy conditions it is advisable that the location be sheltered or that a small pit be dug to contain it, although exposure to a light breeze is good because it will help to start and maintain the fire. First place the tinder on the ground, a handful is enough. Ensure that the tinder is loose and well aerated; tease out dry grass to allow air to flow through it rather than around it. Closely packed tinder will inhibit air flow and cause poor, smoky burning. Then, carefully arrange the kindling on the tinder. Again, a handful is enough, it must not be so heavy that it squashes the teased-out tinder. The kindling can be placed in the form of a cone or in crossways layers, but it is important that the structure be open and well aerated.

As an option, a few thin, flat pieces of bark can be placed to encourage air flow into the base of the fuel, to make the fire catch and burn more readily. Although they may burn later on, these pieces of bark are not part of the fuel, they form a structure that helps to start the fire. If there is a breeze, lay one or a few flat pieces of bark against the kindling to form a sort of half "tepee" structure. Only place the bark in an up-wind position; the breeze will cause turbulence around the pieces of bark, and air will curl around them and into the fire. If there is no breeze, construct a loose cone of bark to form a crude "chimney" by arranging it so that large spaces are left around the base of the fire, with the bark coming closer together at the top of the structure. Do this carefully so as not to put pressure on the fire; it is important that the weight of these bits of bark rests on the ground, not on the kindling and tinder.

Leave all remaining fuel to one side until the fire has been lit, do not just pile it all on at once.

Lighting and fuelling the fire

Now light the fire. Apply a match to the base of the tinder, on the up-wind side only. Allow the breeze to carry the flames into the tinder and kindling. Creating a breeze by blowing on the fire or fanning it with your hat is no substitute for a structure that is freely aerated. Watch how the bark "chimney" is working; if a lot of smoke is being produced it may be necessary to open the base a bit to let more air in, but generally, the less the structure is disturbed after lighting the better.

Allow the fire to burn until the kindling is well alight before adding more fuel. The presence of flames alone does not indicate that the kindling is burning solidly, there must be small red coals forming and significant heat being produced. Next, carefully add the smaller sticks. At this stage the fire is still fragile so be sure not to overburden it with weight, try to maintain an open structure with good air flow into the base of it.

When the small sticks are well alight and producing coals add larger sticks, then some of the bigger bits of wood. It is always best to allow good coals to form before adding the next lot of fuel. Patience at this stage will allow strong combustion to develop with an ability to set fire to the larger pieces of wood that follow.

To boil a billy

For non-Australians, a "billy" is a container much like a pot or saucepan, sometimes just a large tin can with a wire handle attached to two holes made in its top. A billy-boiling fire is a quick one that will not be needed for long. What is needed most is flames, so that direct conduction of heat can occur from the flames to the billy surface. Build a small fire, using mostly thin, small sticks, and if there is any wind make use of it to direct the flames onto the billy. This fire will need regular stoking with increments of small pieces of fuel to maintain the flames at their best. A benefit of a small fast fire is that it will burn out quickly after use and so be easy to extinguish and render safe.

The billy must be positioned right in the flames. The flames should impinge mostly upon the area of the billy that contains the water, which will be the lower parts. If there is a good breeze the billy can be placed on a small elevation such that the flames blow directly onto it, and even under it. Ensure that the billy handle is laid over to the side away from the flames to keep it cooler, which will make it easier to remove after it has boiled. In still conditions with flames going directly upwards a tripod will be more effective. Place the lid on the billy for more rapid boiling but only rest it on, do not jam it on or it will be difficult to remove later when you want to add the tea.

Do not remove a billy lid or the billy itself from the fire by its handle using your unprotected finger, or you may receive a nasty burn and perhaps drop the billy and scald someone. Never use a length of stick either, as this may break under the weight of the billy. Simply use a small piece of wood placed directly on top of your finger as an insulator, to protect you from the heat in the metal handle. When the billy boils add your tea, then remove the billy from the fire immediately or it will froth up and boil over. Allow the tea to brew in a warm spot beside the fire. Gum leaves are optional; as I see it they are just a gimmick and add nothing to the brew.

For evening meals and camp ovens

When cooking a meal in the evening or just sitting around the campfire a longer burning, hotter fire is needed. Cooking on such a fire is different from quickly boiling a billy because the cooking fire employs radiant heat from very hot coals, rather than heat from direct conduction by flames. This requires careful selection of wood that will burn down to produce abundant hot coals. These are usually larger pieces of dense, heavy, dry timber. Local people know which trees supply this kind of wood, they call it "good burning" wood. When the fire is well alight gradually add this wood and allow it to burn fiercely until a bed of coals of the desired size is produced.

Camp ovens need a flat bed of coals to stand on. Scrape a few coals out to the side of the fire for this, the main bed of coals will be far too hot. Coals can also be put onto the lid to provide all-round heating. The heat of the oven can be regulated by placing more, or less, coals upon the lid, and occasionally replacing the coals underneath. It is handy to carry a small garden trowel to use for this purpose.

Barbeque plates, tripods, etc. can also be used on such a fire.

Construction of a tripod

In still conditions a tripod is an effective tool for holding a billy. It can also be useful over a cooking fire. A temporary tripod can be made on the spot from three lengths of green wood. One is cut so that it has a short branch which points towards the stem of the stick, and the other two have a small fork at one end pointing away from the stem. The first of these is stood upside down on the ground so that it's small branch points towards the ground. The forks of the other two are then meshed with the branch of the first one to form a sturdy tripod. The billy can then be hung from one of the forks.

A permanent tripod can easily be constructed from three lengths of steel rod and a piece of chain consisting of only three links. The two end-links of the chain are welded longitudinally onto the end sections of two of the rods, and the third (centre) link is welded transversely across the end of the middle piece. Tie on a hook to support the billy. This tripod is very strong and will fold neatly and completely. When the tripod is no longer needed, push it over onto the ground to allow it to cool before stowage. It can be stored in a length of plastic drainpipe with reinforced ends, so that carbon black from the tripod does not contaminate other items in the load when in transit or storage.

A smokeless fire

The essence of a smokeless fire is good aeration of the fuel so that it can burn completely, as measured by the vigour of the flames it produces. A billy-boiling fire built as described above will be smokeless, as it is made with small, readily burnable sticks and is very well aerated, producing abundant flames. The flames ensure that all combustible materials produced are fully burnt, leaving only invisible gasses.

If the fuel in a fire is laid too densely or is at all wet, it will not burn rapidly or produce good flames. Combustion will be incomplete, and smoke will be produced as a result. Smoke is a mixture of gasses and particulate matter that have been produced by heat but have not been completely burnt. A fire can be made to produce smoke as a signal by piling a dense layer of green foliage such as leaves or grass on top of it.

If you have no matches

Aboriginal populations around the world have devised various ways of making a fire without the benefit of matches. Some carried red hot coals with them. But one of the most reliable items for making fire has five parts. The first is a bow, or a small length of strong but pliable wood with a roughly semi-circular shape, cut from a branch of a tree. The second part is a length of strong cord; I use a long leather bootlace. Then there is a shaft, a straight piece of hard wood with a sharpened end, which is to be turned by the bow. The cord is tied to each end of the bow, but loosely, so that the shaft can be included in a twist of it. A flat capstone with a shallow recess in it is used to hold against the top of the shaft as it is turned by the bow, and below the bottom of the shaft is a piece of soft, dry wood.

In operation, the cord of the bow is twisted around the shaft. The shaft is placed in a vertical position, the bottom of it resting on the piece of soft dry wood. One's left hand holds the capstone against the top of it. The right hand holds the bow in a horizontal position, and pushing it forwards and pulling it back causes the shaft to twirl in one direction and then the other. The action is similar to using an old-fashioned hand drill, but the "bow" is moved back and forth, rather than round and round like the handle of a drill.

A simple magnifying glass can also be used to focus the rays of the sun.

How to extinguish a fire

It is important to keep control of a fire and not allow it to escape into the bush. Before you leave a campfire, it is best to pull out the bigger pieces of wood and extinguish them first. Then push the smaller sticks right into the fire and let them burn completely It is safer to burn a campfire out completely than to leave it smouldering. Lastly, completely bury the fire, so that even if a wind comes up no hot embers can be blown away from it.

The Kimberley competition

I once judged a competition between four men who had been too long in the bush. The competition was to see who could boil a billy in the shortest possible time. This was held at the height of the dry season in a remote part of the Australian Kimberley and became such an obsession that for some time it was held annually.

Rules were devised for this spectacular event. The contestants were allowed to collect as much fuel as they wanted, construct their fire, and fill their billy with a prescribed amount of water. They were also allowed to place their billy where they wanted it to be, but they were not allowed to actually start the fire. There was a lot of variation in technique. Some collected quite substantial pieces of wood, and some stockpiled only small sticks. The interesting thing was the placement of the billys. One man placed his billy on the ground about 30 centimetres directly down-wind from his fire, and we were very curious as to why. Then, with matches in hand, the four of them lined up behind the starting line. Only one match was to be used, and a penalty was applied for every additional one.

Upon the word "Go!" they shot off towards their fires, striking matches as they went. All the fires were quickly ablaze as the fuel was very dry indeed. Then we appreciated the strategy of the man who had placed his billy so far down-wind from his fire. The wind was quite strong and blew the flames into a frenzy, so that each fire acted like a veritable blowtorch. The billy placed 30 centimetres from the fire was right at the hottest point of this blowtorch, and it boiled in one minute forty seconds flat. He won the competition!

Part II

A Taxi Through Phnom Penh
And Other Tales

John Aldrick

An assortment of short stories about travel in many countries, true, unique and humorous, seen through the eyes of an Australian.

Author's Note

The stories in Part II are derived from the author's experiences travelling and working in many different countries throughout the underdeveloped world. His travels have given him unique glimpses into many cultures, and an insight into their daily lives and conditions. His work has called for travelling in vehicles and aircraft that were in dubious condition or essentially unserviceable, in yak carts, by donkey, on foot, and has involved him in military coups, striplines in tropical forest, haircuts in strange places, foreign languages, human hazards, volcanic eruptions, typhoons, earthquakes, the vagaries of 100cc motorbikes, and he was once nearly shipwrecked. They range from episodes with crocodiles, bears, cobras, pigs, hyenas, vultures and bandits, to the perils of going to the toilet.

Apart from small changes to disguise personal identities or provide continuity these stories are all true.

Contents

A taxi through Phnom Penh	113
Face first down the mountain	115
My haircut in Saigon	119
A Himalayan bear in Bhutan	121
Flying in New Guinea and such places	128
A Hash House Harriers cobra	134
The perils of going to the toilet	138
Overnight in Calcutta	140
The Great Rift Valley and Addis Ababa	143
Camping out in Timor	147
Cocoa, taro and beetles in Rabaul	151
Landing at Mount Hagen	158
A military coup in Ethiopia	159
Insurgents, militias and human hazards	163
Almost shipwrecked off Sumbawa	168
Strip-lines, tropical forest and mangroves	172
My crop of marijuana	178
Law and order in Manila	180
I lost a man in Aitape	181
That elusive door	185
My boss in Indonesia	187
A GPS at Bewani River	188
A little foreign language is not enough	192
We broke the helicopter's tail boom	196

Accommodation in Sagaranten 201
By donkey to a Himalayan school 207

Bonus: Tips for travelling in
underdeveloped countries 211
This bonus is a valuable supplement to the information distributed with passport renewals or by travel agents and insurance companies. It is specifically for travel in under-developed countries, or remote areas where the normal facilities of the big cities are primitive or non-existent.

A taxi through Phnom Penh

Taxis have a habit of being interestingly different across the globe, but I think that the most grippingly unnerving of all is the 100cc motorbike. These bikes are almost universal in underdeveloped countries and are used for many forms of transport. Taking goods to and from a marketplace is one of them. They can carry a whole family, commonly four or five people, I've sometimes seen six on one; dad drives, mum sits behind him and carries the baby, one child sits on the petrol tank in front of dad and another perches on the handlebars, and the last sits on the parcel carrier at the rear. With only two or three on board the lady often sits side-saddle, her slippers dangling casually from her toes, and I have never seen a slipper fall off.

I have been a passenger on these things many times. On one occasion, I had been to see a senior public servant in the city of Phnom Penh to enquire about obtaining some aerial photographs. There were some language difficulties, I never could master a tonal language. I gathered that I had to send a fax to an agency in Bangkok requesting the photographs. "You must send a fuk (sic) to Bangkok" she kept informing me, loudly and earnestly. So, cogitating upon this seemingly superfluous piece of advice, I hailed a taxi to return to my hotel, which was also the location of my office.

Taxis in Cambodia are the usual 100cc motorbikes, the drivers of which see you on the footpath and slow right down and run along beside you, usually with a tout upon the back, never mind if it's the wrong side of the road. The tout got off and I boarded this one, then the tout got back on again behind me. The driver roared off instantly, never mind where to, the important thing was to get this important foreigner there, wherever it was, fast. Hanging on, I reached forward and held a picture of my hotel in front of the driver, he saw it, and being very quick on the uptake he did a nimble U-turn through four lanes of traffic and shot off towards it, albeit again on the wrong side of the road. That was OK so far, one gets used to this, the crucial thing is to hang on, because these manoeuvres are unpredictable and counter-intuitive for us Westerners and it is easy to lose one's balance, let alone one's nerve.

We reached the turnoff to my hotel and were rattling down the verge of a very rough and pot-holed dirt track, at the end of which was my hotel, a new four-star place; I guess the land there was going cheap. After a little bit of footpath work, dodging pedestrians, and trying to get in front of a bullock cart, there loomed in front of us a roadside stall. Like many Asian cities, free enterprise reigns in Phnom Penh, in other words, if you don't look after yourself no-one else will. There are hosts of little roadside stalls of every description lining the smaller streets which carry mostly foot traffic, and so reasonable sales are there to be made. One such stall was just ahead of us, charcoal fire burning, soup simmering, nameless things sizzling in a pan, and an awning up to shelter patrons from the sun.

Out of nowhere a large truck appeared, lumbering unconcernedly along in front of us and also about to pass the roadside stall, but there was no room for us in between. My driver was faced with the prospect of slowing down, but he was having none of that, you don't slow down in Asia. So he changed down a gear, accelerated, and sounding his feeble cicada-like horn he aimed straight at the space beneath the stall's small awning.

I was head and shoulders taller than either the driver or his tout, and whilst I imagine they could easily have passed underneath that awning, I, clinging on grimly, looking at the prospect, was damn sure that I could not. I suppose that there was quite a lot of room really, but by this time I calculated that I had run out of options. We couldn't return to the road, the truck was there. We couldn't stop, we were going too fast. We were committed to the space reserved for the normal customers of the stall.

By this time I could see right over the top of the awning which was approaching very rapidly, so I ducked and cringed with all my might, and with a small eddy of wind and a little puff of raised dust we shot underneath that awning and out the other side, myself intact, but I tell you what, it didn't do a lot for my continence.

My driver and his tout were unperturbed, they interpreted my reaction as quite normal under the circumstances, they would have done the same in my position, they faced that kind of thing every day. The owner of the stall was also sanguine, nothing had been spilt and there were no customers anyway, so why not let the space be used? All we had done was frighten a couple of his chooks.

Somewhat shaken and slightly rattled, I paid the driver the equivalent of twenty cents. Now that is cheap, for a ride you couldn't buy in Luna Park!

Face first down the mountain

There is more than one way to descend from a mountain range, as I discovered, and upon one's face is one of them. I was in a lovely traditional village on a broad, forested mountain ridge in Mindanao, and now I had to descend from the mountain to get back to the world below. I'd come up here two days before to undertake a study project and had spent a quite fantastic time communicating with the village people. They were Lumads, the semi-nomadic indigenous inhabitants of those mountains. I'd stayed overnight in the village. A cottage owner had vacated her bed for me because it was the only one with a mosquito net. The others slept on the floor on mats, with just a blanket for warmth. It was a bit of a risk for me because there were all sorts of rebels, bandits, and dissidents in those areas and as a European I would have been a perfect hostage for ransom if I was caught.

Now, we were about to go down. Our taxis had arrived, just as ordered, two of them, both 100cc motorbikes. That was OK because there were only five of us, at least in the official party, although there were some opportunists waiting in the wings. They knew that if they could sneak a ride with us they wouldn't have to walk all the way down the mountain.

And so we boarded, parted from our friends and colleagues, and began our downhill run. It was actually quite smooth at first, no hurry. There were only three on my motorbike, although I suspect there might have been a fourth at times hitch-hiking on the rear parcel carrier. The other bike had a varying number of passengers, mostly four but sometimes five. There's more room than you think on a 100cc motorbike. But I was not adequately aware that it takes a lot more to stop a motorbike going down than it takes to drive one uphill.

It was an actual road, never properly formed, just more or less hewn out from the mountain side with at least some consideration for gradient and drainage. I knew it well, I had travelled on it on my way up, and once was quite enough to know that road. I felt prepared for all that might eventuate, no problem really, I was quite relaxed, accepting whatever my fate might be. But what I didn't fully realize at first was that it was now downhill, and it was very steep.

We joggled on, quite quickly at first, at 15 or 20 kilometres per hour I should think. The bike was quite a small one and we had to help the driver balance, for the road was rough and steep and tortuous. On my taxi, front to back in order, there were the driver, then me, and behind me was my counterpart and guide, a short and dumpy woman but very able and alert. She hung onto me, I hung onto the driver, and he hung onto his 100cc motorbike. And so we progressed, rattling down that mountain.

And then we hit a bump, just one of many, and I felt my counterpart's grip upon me slacken. In fact, she just let go. I thought OK, she's busy doing something. Casually I looked around and noticed to my surprise that she was completely off the bike, about 20 metres behind it in fact, and running flat out down the slope behind it. I mused; why is she doing that? She was an intelligent woman, not given to impetuous acts. It seemed quite curious, after all, she had a perfectly good seat upon our motorbike. Why was she now back up there behind us, running? She was fairly pelting down that slope, with a look of concentration on her face.

At first I felt upset, there she was, having exercise and fun, without inviting me! It took some time, but then I realized that on that bump she'd been evicted, thrown right off the motorbike, and the purpose of her running was to keep herself upright until she slowed sufficiently to stabilize herself. Arms flailing, head back, legs pistoning, she was running as a desperado, full tilt down behind the motorbike. At my last sight of her she was clearly slowing down, and I felt sure that she would make it.

But then we hit another bump, and the bike bucked me off also. I wasn't quite as good as her, I missed my cue, I didn't have the wit to start out running too. Instead I soared, and fell into the roadside ditch, it was a sort of drain, and I lobbed there horizontally, completely on my face, and at quite a pace.

It wasn't such a bad drain really, it was wet and not so rocky, and I slid quite easily down the mountain slope. I had a close-up view of all the sandy bits and stones, right there before my face, moving fast towards me like some electronic play screen. And then there were the puddles; I hit them far too fast and cast a spray about, the silty water stung my eyes, but I continued on, I had no choice. I went quite fast, in fact I'm sure that once I overtook my 100cc motorbike.

As I descended down that gutter, quite unperturbed, I observed the plants beside the ditch. The forest had been cleared, which mostly leads to soil erosion on such steep slopes, leaving only re-growth scrub. As I rasped along the ditch I observed the land and cogitated; I thought that it was fine, that all this re-growth was preventing soil erosion, it was actually quite good. I hadn't thought of it before, as now, from down below, I hadn't had a close-up chance, as a scientist, quite like this. I was in an analytical state of mind, as I shot down in that drain. So I travelled on, as I had to, down that vagrant gutter.

But then I focused, there was a bend, and I was sliding straight towards it. Would I be capable of navigating it? I'd had no practice at this sort of thing, in roadside drains. Maybe I could sluice around it toboggan-wise, or perhaps I would just mount the bank and shoot up in the scrub? My capacity to steer was not so good.

But no, we all had slowed. The bike had stopped, my counterpart as well, she was panting, somewhat agog, beside the motorbike, and I myself had pulled down to a halt. I got up from the ditch, scraped sand and gravel from my front, wiped mud and leaves from off my face and re-joined them, at the 100cc motorbike.

Without a word, not a murmur, we boarded once again, and headed on down further. No word was said, no apprehension felt, it was just another thing. But on our way, as we descended, it occurred to me that no-one thought it strange. That woman, belting down the slope behind; and myself, my face inside the ditch, roaring down the drain. But most of all what did intrigue me was our calm acceptance of it, it was just a normal way to travel. That was just the way that one descended, from that mountain range.

My haircut in Saigon

I had to have a haircut. I have had them in various places, but you do tend to remember some more than others. Hazard is built into some of them, but maybe bliss in others.

There was one, with me seated on a packing case on a footpath in Kupang. There was a retinue around me, intrigued by my grey hair, picking up bits of it from the footpath and offering encouragement to the barber to get more active and hack me back a bit more, so that they could all have some. That haircut came to a speedy end when the barber went back inside his "shop", indulged in a serious bout of coughing, then re-emerged, saying (in Indonesian) "excuse me sir, it's my AIDS". Not that I think it was, but I bolted anyway.

I had a rather frustrating haircut in Bangkok when a woman hairdresser in a hotel complex wanted to trim off my sideburns, and made a horizontal cut across them just above my ears, quite against my express wishes and the normal trim of my whiskers. She and I had a difference of opinion about it, me being emphatic and she being persistent. She asked, why would I want to go against the prevailing fashion? After some animated discussion we compromised, which meant she eventually got her way and did it anyway, bit by bit, by stealth. If you ever want to see something funny it would be me with a Chinese haircut.

Mostly, in Asia, a man wanting a haircut gets a homosexual doing it for him. They seem to think that men feel more important if a man attends to him, some sort of superiority. But these "men" in all the barber shops are just the same. Why not a woman, given the sheer loveliness of some of these Asian ones, and if it must be a man why a homosexual, of all people? The usual scenario when you need a haircut is that you first find a barber shop. All the hair-cutting personnel on display are women. Expectantly, you walk inside, then those lovely women retire and drag out the homosexual, and he comes greasing up to you, folding his towel over his arm and extinguishing his cigarette.

But the haircut I prized most of all would have to be the one I had in Saigon. I knew there was a barber shop in my street as I had been past it before, and in these places, one tends to make a mental note of such things. One day I fronted up there for a haircut. The shop was just off the street, about two metres back from the traffic. This time it was a very different experience. I was the only customer. There were three young women hair cutters in there. All were probably 18-20 year olds, hard to tell with Vietnamese, and all were quite beautiful; slender, stylish, well-proportioned and full of smiles. I really was the guest of honour. I was ushered to my seat by all three of them, smiled at, patted, and almost caressed along the way. I sat down in the chair. Surely, any minute now, they would bring out the homosexual? But no, that didn't happen. What followed first was a whole heap of giggles, as my hair was closely inspected and felt by all three of them. Asians aren't used to grey hair and I guess they felt unsure as to how to proceed. They were really very polite giggles.

The process took about an hour. Gently, carefully, with unreal dexterity and precision and with total respect and deference, they cut off my hair. One cut off the main part on the top of my head, the bit I had walked in there for. Another took out all the hair inside my ears and nostrils, and the third did the same with my neck and sought around for more. All the while they clucked together musically, with graceful movements and laughter, like a trio of elegant hens, clearly enjoying and devoted to their work. Smiling into my face, their thirty delicate little fingers then thoroughly searched my head, checking for any residual hairiness. I felt like a king.

At the end, they opened the door to let me out because it was air-conditioned in there, not that I was too willing to leave mind you, and I enquired about the fee. I was asked for it in Dong, the Vietnamese currency, a paltry amount, just cents to us, given that a wheelbarrow-full is needed for most transactions. I had been so well treated and felt so good about my haircut that I gave them ten-fold, and in US dollars, still very little for me but probably a month's worth of Dong to them.

Not a lot wrong with that for a haircut! I felt that in my fantasy, I would have taken any one of those truly lovely women back home with me, or to anywhere in the world, for life, purely to cut my hair of course.

A Himalayan bear in Bhutan

Bhutan is an amazing country. The first time I went there we landed at Paro airport, which is in the next valley over from the capital town, Timphu. The airport is at Paro because that valley contains the only reasonably long flat stretch of land. Immigration and customs services are undertaken in a little hut off to one side, the only building there, but I didn't know that, and there were no signs of any sort. I actually walked in there trying to find someone to stamp my passport, a man behind a desk looked at me, but there seemed to be no activity, so I walked out again, guessing that these functions would be carried out in Timphu. So I boarded the bus to Timphu, but there were no formalities there either, so I went to my hotel and checked in. Some days later when I was already far away in the east of the country the authorities discovered that I was an illegal immigrant, and they were waiting for me when I returned to

Timphu. Beaming with bonhomie, they threatened me with all sorts of official reprisals and then offered me a cup of Bhutanese tea, which I considered to be punishment enough, and welcomed me to Bhutan; after all, it was more their fault than mine.

The aircraft I flew on was a Dornier, a German built utility model and generally pretty spartan, with about twenty steel-framed canvas seats. It had Lycoming engines, which were a bit of a worry as they were well known to throw crankshafts. It was a spectacular flight, starting in Calcutta on the Ganges delta, then going obliquely along the Ganges River and over its junction with the Brahma Putra, both of them huge rivers, a visual feast for a geomorphologist like me. Then the Himalayas stood up from the plains in front of us like a huge wall, as the plane laboured for more and more height. They flew that plane like a helicopter, winding up the mountain valleys towards Paro, struggling for elevation, because Paro airport is higher than Australia's Mount Kosciusko. At times one felt almost able to reach out and grab a handful of snow from a passing bluff. Sometimes they couldn't make it through the mountains because of bad visibility and had to return, usually to Dhaka, and wait for better weather in the mountains; that only happened to me once.

When my work in Bhutan was over and I was returning to India I couldn't board the aircraft for an hour or so after the scheduled take-off time, because it was the first aircraft the Bhutanese people had ever owned, in fact their first airline, and lots of dignitaries and their friends and relations wanted to go up for joyrides over Timphu. I guess it was their aircraft! I heard that they eventually crashed it, bought a new type of aircraft, and began using Bangkok as their foreign service port.

My job as a consultant was to check out a string of locations for the prospects of irrigating rice. There was plenty of water but not much good land because most of it was steeply sloping, as one would expect in the Himalayas. The only land with any prospect at all was on the old alluvial terraces and fans of the many rivers which only flowed spasmodically, but even these strips of land were sloping at about ten percent. The soils were quite coarse and sandy and inherently susceptible to severe erosion, so any irrigation had to be on man-made levelled terraces. Soil infiltration rates were high and "puddling" of the soils to reduce infiltration was a necessity. Organic matter was an annual requirement, and it was interesting to see the small regularly spaced heaps of dung spread out across the cultivated fields to fertilize the soil by the women cleaning out the stables, where the farm animals had been housed during the long cold winter, by carrying it out on their heads in large circular baskets.

My work took me right across to the eastern side of Bhutan, past Mongar and the many mad dogs of Tashigang, almost to the border with the Indian Province of Assam, travelling on Himalayan mountain roads. I had hired a beat-up old Toyota Land Cruiser and a "mountain" driver, so classified because he was able to avoid becoming dizzy even though the roads were so winding that he spent half his time peering through the side window at the other side of the many hairpin bends. He had a huge wobbly plastic bag full of petrol tied to the roof rack, as fuel supplies were hard to come by where we were going. The driver had an unnerving habit of throwing the vehicle out of gear and coasting down the mountain slopes with all their hairpin bends to "save petrol", despite the potential of that plastic bag should it rupture, and relying solely on the brakes to pull us up. He inspected the brake linings every evening, they were perilously thin.

We drove across the top of the country, over snow covered mountain passes at 15,000 feet with only Rhododendrons and conifers, down some of the most difficult roads and tracks I have ever been on. Landslips and rock falls onto the road were common. Once I dropped a stone over a vertical cliff and timed its descent – it took four seconds until the first bounce. That's a long way down! At each prospective irrigation site we left the vehicle, took up all our gear and walked up into the hills for several days of work on foot, staying in the villages that were there. Once, my equipment was carried up the slope by a hefty, rosy cheeked sixteen year old girl, her baby slung in a fabric cradle on her back and suspended on a strap across the top of her forehead. She was almost running up the slope, and I, fit as I was and unladen, stumbled and struggled to keep up. But not all the people are as fit. It takes two men to operate a shovel in Bhutan. The blade is worn down to about half its original length. One man pushes the gnarled and worn handle, and the other pulls with a rope tied around the base of it. It's quite an art, they have to coordinate and work together to be successful.

Whilst out there, I had to send a message back to Calcutta. I wrote it, and sought the postal service, which was just one man, he was the Post Office. This man was fit, no Ethiopian marathon runner could have competed with him. I gave him money for a stamp, but he wouldn't accept any more for food along the way. He put my note in the cleft of a small stick and held it above his head as if it was a piece of gold, and then he started to run. A hundred and fifty kilometres before him to Timphu, and then back again. I felt so inadequate; I had just come down that road by 4WD motor vehicle, right along the middle of the Himalayas. He was fed and watered automatically by people everywhere along his path, as still he ran, some ran beside him for a while, in a token of recognition and respect. And that man ran for three days; my lone message always up above his head, because he was the normal cross-mountain mail. In Timphu, he bought the stamp and stuck it onto my letter with the pot of glue provided. And when he came back, he showed me his empty cleft stick to indicate that the job had been done, like a receipt, and gave me my change from the money for the stamp. I offered him food and drink, but he wouldn't take any, he said that he had his work to go to. And later, I found that my letter had duly arrived in Calcutta.

There were a lot of accidents and injuries amongst the people. It was an 18th Century civilisation and life was pretty tough. I treated one young woman who had a rock fall on her head as she walked along a mountain path. Her brain was exposed, and because of that the locals had given her up as lost, but I gave her first aid and packed her off in my vehicle with my driver back to Tashigang, and I heard later that she did recover. But without my transport I had to walk 15 kilometres back to my abode, at night, in the dark, through the mountains, past several rabid dogs. I reached my place at dawn, just as my driver returned. At another time, I treated a man for a deep wound to his groin, exposing the femoral artery. He had been gored by one of the Mithun bulls he had been ploughing with and was losing a lot of blood. These bulls are huge, and after a day's work they are really cranky, and taking off their yokes can be quite dangerous. I dusted sulphanilamide into the wound and bound it to reduce the bleeding, but I doubt he would have survived.

The food was interesting. Mostly it was boiled cabbage and rice for every meal, three times a day, and if you were lucky there may be a chilli. I carried a tin of sausages from India with me for a long time but when I finally opened it in great anticipation I found that it was nearly all water, with just a small amount of fatty sausage. What a disappointment! Eggs are regarded as a delicacy in Bhutan, and it is customary when one arrives at a village to be met by a dignitary and his entourage, with a plate of boiled eggs. On this occasion they knew of our arrival long before we got there and were all assembled and prepared. I had to eat a "welcome" egg, but it was cracked and most definitely off, it tasted foul, but there was no way I could refuse. After several hours, I really had a dose of vomiting and diarrhoea.

Apart from the roads, the most dangerous part of my job was the prospect of meeting a Himalayan Black Bear whilst walking along the narrow paths and tracks. They were terrible and dangerous animals, almost as big as a Grizzly, black, but with a white collar around their throat, and they struck great fear into the locals. There was a sort of pattern to their attacks. People would come across these bears unexpectedly around a bend in the track, and the bear, quick to be enraged, would rush up and grab them, roar into their ears, give them a brief mauling to go on with, and then, for some unknown reason, tear off their scalp and let them go. At certain times of year, the hospital in Bhutan had a regular clientele of unfortunates who had lost their scalp or had perhaps presented holding it in their hands. And so it was with some trepidation that I trod those mountain tracks myself.

I was out upon the job, on foot, right away towards the east, past Tashigang, covering up to 25 kilometres a day, investigating the irrigation potential of a number of small patches of land. I was camped inside a Nepalese labourer's hut where I stored my gear and slept at night. My mentor gathered food for me from the local village. The hut was built of plaited split bamboo mats cast upon a bamboo frame, with two layers on the roof for better water-proofing. There was no door, just an opening, and a bamboo mat to prop against it when I went to bed at night. My bed was a bamboo platform built a little above the ground, and on it I slept inside my sleeping bag of warm and cozy down.

My hut was on a shallow mountain dome, the roof of the world, with wild strawberries as the only plants. My "office" was a small folding card table and a stool just outside the hut, and there I used my high-tech optical stereoscope to interpret aerial photographs of my work areas and to document my findings. From that lofty perch outside my hut I had a most magnificent view. I could look up and see the incredible, jagged, Tibetan Plateau, and looking down I could see the very tops of thunderstorms in the valleys below, with dull orange flashes as lightning played inside them, and at night the faint twinkling lights of India far away.

On this particular night I went to bed, all seemed secure, no problems there, but I had forgotten to close my door; that little piece of bamboo mat was still propped beside the wall near the entrance, not placed to block the opening. I realised this quite soon, when I was awakened by a sound. A sound of gnashing, "tush, tush, tush", and I froze inside my sleeping bag. As I had woken, unthinking, I had raised my hand, and accidentally touched and felt the warm and shaggy coat of a large and hairy animal. It was definitely right there inside my hut, just beside my sleeping bag, and I was in there with it! I had not closed my door, and panic! It would have to be a Himalayan bear! It was right there, standing just beside me! I cringed, expecting every minute was my last, and to feel great teeth upon my throat, and those fearful claws ripping off my scalp.

But nothing happened; the noise went on, in episodes of repetition. It would be there now, then not, then it would begin again. The noise began once more, a repetitious crunching sound, I was sure it was a bear gnashing its teeth preparatory to dealing me a blow. And after what seemed like aeons of time with no result, from inside my sleeping bag I carefully switched on my torch. A large and hairy beast was definitely right there beside me! Just half a metre away! But do you know, as my eyes began to focus, with my torch now fully on, I saw that it was just a cow. The cow, quite used to being shedded for the winter, had seen my open door and walked inside, grateful for the warmth and shelter, and the sound that I had heard was the chewing of her cud!

Flying in New Guinea and such places

I had to meet a plane that was bringing me supplies, and also a surveyor from Port Moresby who was coming to assist me, at a remote place in the north of Papua New Guinea between Aitape and Wewak. It was a hastily constructed old wartime strip, very long and wide, floored with interlocking sheets of steel mesh (Marsden matting) but quite without regular maintenance. I knew where the strip was because I had aerial photographs, but you would never have suspected its presence from what passed for a road along the coast beside it. There was no clear access to this airstrip, one needed four-wheel drive and had to travel through the bush to get to it. But I knew the route, I had travelled it at intervals before.

Tracks in PNG are always recognizable by their cleavage through the forest, never mind the shrubs and herbs, they grow all the time, but if you see that the trees have been removed there is quite likely to have been a track, and it may still be possible to drive through there. This particular track was like that, always wet, barely passable, with wheel tracks almost axle deep. There was one sharp bend upon that track that always caused me strife. As I struggled on towards that old airstrip I came again upon that bend, I knew it well, there was an overhanging tree that kept forcing me out into a bog beside the track. Time was running out. I turned around in the driver's seat and said to my crew of PNG locals, because one always addressed them collectively, and then they sort it out amongst themselves; "One pella, kissim bushknife, chopim DY" which was understood to mean one of you get out and prune that tree. One man did, and on we went.

We arrived beside the strip. The plane coming in was a Twin Otter. The pilot landed with one flat tyre and on only one engine. I pointed to the tyre, but he just shrugged, so I asked about the engine and he shrugged again; he still had one of each left. His main concern seemed to be whether I could charge his almost flat battery. I couldn't do that in the bush, so he left the remaining engine running while we unloaded, and then he prepared to take off again, regardless. The plane accelerated, travelling fairly straight down the strip, I think the drag of the flat tyre on one side was counterbalanced by the sideways pull of the remaining engine on the other. He seemed to think it was a fair thing, but thank goodness I was not on board.

There was another Twin Otter though, and I was destined to board this one. It came in to Aitape "airport" more or less on schedule. However, there was a delay in getting it going again and for the life of me I couldn't see why. For some obscure reason they were piling all the people they could muster into the rear cargo hold, even onto the tail wing, and taking all the weight they could off the front. There were plenty of willing and enthusiastic bystanders, as is usual anywhere in PNG, where nothing much changes but the numbers of pigs and dogs. They thought it was marvellous fun and probably not far short of a cargo cult sort of thing. Then the plane shifted visibly; it sat back on its haunches just a little, and the nose wheel almost left the ground.

Then there was action! The pilot, an Australian chap, got a sort of crank handle, and right up front he began to turn it, and as he did the nose wheel slowly revolved until it was facing straight ahead. Then they removed the throng, they all got off, weight was restored to the front wheel, and with an audible clack the nose wheel locked itself into the straight-ahead position. Apparently, a control cable had snapped on landing, and it was no longer possible for the pilot to steer the aircraft whilst it was on the ground.

Now I have to tell you that the airport "terminal" at Aitape is fairly primitive. It's a tin shed like a small garden shed, similar to the old one at Borroloola in Australia. Its main distinguishing feature was a sign upon one wall, not far different from some sorts of graffiti, that proclaimed the virtues of the local airline with the words "We Specialize In Airfrighting". It was pretty pertinent too, they did. But the Twin Otter was faced directly front-on to the terminal and right up close to it, so it couldn't move forwards or turn. It was then that I learned something about Twin Otters; that they could power out backwards, simply by reversing the pitch on the propeller blades.

So, we boarded. The pilot backed right out to the runway, which stood at right angles to us. But then we had to take off, and I was wondering how he planned to do it. You can't take planes off sideways with any real degree of confidence, even in New Guinea. But he was more resourceful than I thought. As he reversed, he used the individual wheel brakes to manoeuvre the aircraft until it was pointing more or less down the strip, I guess it was only a matter of 10 or 12 degrees off course. Then he opened up the throttles and we headed for the scrub, missed it by a good couple of metres, and he used the foot brakes and the tailplane (once we had airspeed) to pull it into line and aim it down the rest of the strip. And so, we took off. Now isn't that ingenious?

One plane was running a sort of "milk run" around the foothills to the north of the main Highlands, and I was going all the way to the last stop, Vanimo, near the Irian Jaya border. The plane was fully loaded, the central seats occupied by women nursing pigs, the children sitting on the floor with the baggage. There were some hairy landings. At one place I couldn't see the strip at all, although the pilot was clearly slowing down and lowering flaps in preparation for a landing. We banked sharply to the left, passing just between a low rocky knoll and some trees, then immediately past that we banked even more sharply to the right and the plane dipped steeply down, and then I saw the strip. It was just a short one, more or less straight, with what appeared to be a small creek flowing across its middle. The pilot put it down hard, right at the start of the strip, applied full reverse pitch and brakes, spray went flying as we crossed the creek, and we stopped just short of the end of the runway. I guess it was fail-safe because beyond the strip was an almost vertical drop, and if we couldn't have stopped in time, with a bit of luck, the pilot could have gone around power and used that drop to get the plane airborne again. It seemed to be all in the day's work for him.

It reminded me a bit of a flight I had from Maumere in the island of Flores in Indonesia. The plane was an old ex-military Hawker Sidley, and we were going to Kupang in West Timor. The pilot was a rather attractive young Indonesian woman, clearly under instruction from a more experienced pilot, also Indonesian, who was sitting in the seat beside her. She took off well, and then a strange thing happened. The instructing pilot proceeded to cover all the cockpit windows with newspaper, sealed so that the trainee couldn't see a thing outside the cockpit. She flew it blind on instruments by herself to Kupang, and clearly, she was then supposed to land, still with no outside vision. We passengers could see though, out of the side windows, and it was a bit disconcerting, for the aircraft made several passes over the runway at about 200 feet, all of them at an angle such that if she had actually landed, the runway would have only been briefly crossed; the rest of the landing would have been across the paddock. But then the instructor took pity on her and removed the newspaper and she landed very well, to our relief. I'm not sure that this was legal even in Indonesia with a full complement of passengers on board, but I guess it would have passed scrutiny easily enough in that remote part of the country.

I had climbed aboard another small plane (also a Twin Otter) in Kupang before, it was full of spiders' webs, and there was an unrestrained goat asleep on a pile of baggage at the back. The pilot just started up the engines, revved them up and took off right across the field, straight over the middle of the main runway without looking left or right and flew us on to Ruteng, also in Flores but further to the west. Ruteng is down in the bottom of an old volcanic crater. The pilot was a bit too high on approach, but no problem for him. To descend, he didn't circle gradually down, as would have been conventional. After crossing the rim of the volcano, he pointed the aircraft's nose straight down towards the strip and descended at what seemed to be about 45 degrees. It was a very steep direct descent. Through the front windows I could see the end of the runway rushing up towards us, airframe screaming, and I was sure he'd never pull it out in time and that we were going to crash. But he did, he straightened out at the last minute and made a perfect landing, gently and securely on the end of the runway. They don't fly planes for the comfort of the passengers in eastern Indonesia, and he was not a man for niceties, that pilot. I was a bit shaken, but the goat must have been used to it because I don't think it woke up during the entire flight.

On the return flight later that day, the cabin was still half full of spiders' webs, two of the passengers were perched on top of big boxes of cargo which were occupying their seats, and the "steward" slept through the whole flight. There were no livestock on board, anyway.

One of the more precarious flights I have had was in Cambodia. We were based in Phnom Penh on a study of part of the Mekong delta, and thought that on the following Sunday, for something interesting to do, we would go to the famous temple of Angkor Wat in the north of the country. One of us was appointed to make the arrangements, and on the day, the five of us assembled at Phnom Penh airport.

The plane was full, there were no spare seats at all, so it was good that we had booked. The plane was an old Russian Tupulov, remarkable for its very high take-off and landing speeds, which is probably why the tyres were so bald. We rocketed down the runway, took off and flew uneventfully to Siam Reap, the airport closest to Angkor, and took a local taxi to the temple (Wat means temple). Angkor Wat was very beautiful, very moving, and worth every bit of our time and effort to see it.

Then it was time for us to return to Siam Reap airport for our flight back to Phnom Penh. We were in the departure lounge, and passengers were streaming in. There seemed to be too many of them for what was only a medium sized plane, and ours was the only flight scheduled to depart, so I did a rough head count. According to me there were several more people than available seats, so I quietly said to my colleagues "don't be last onto this flight!". We boarded, and sure enough eight passengers more than there were seats came aboard. Safety or not, these passengers were instructed to either sit in the aisles and hold onto the seat struts, or stand and "strap-hang", holding on to the overhead lockers. Then we took off.

This procedure was repeated when we approached Phnom Penh to land, but as the plane landed and decelerated one of the strap-hangers lost her grip and catapulted down the aisle. She slid along at quite a rate and took out several people's baggage and one standing man as she went. But that was the least of my worries. Looking out the window I noticed that two fire engines were racing alongside, hosing down the wheels. We heard later that they were cooling off the brakes, and that this was standard practice. Those Tupulovs landed at a very fast speed and they usually overheated their brakes. It was a pretty rough airport.

What a way to see a Wat!

A Hash House Harriers cobra

It was a long weekend in Bangkok and we were at a loose end, so on Friday afternoon we decided to drive down to Pattaya in the south of Thailand. My mate had a car and knew the roads, so off we went. We were both keen Hash House Harriers, members of that world-wide group of people who liked to run. Once a week at least, in almost every part of the globe there is an "HHH" run, and for the aficionados these are not to be missed. There was a Hash House Harriers run scheduled in Pattaya for Saturday, and that was our reason for travelling there, we wanted to be in the run.

I have run the Hash many times, in a number of different countries. The runs are laid out by a person familiar with the area known as the "hare" who lays down a sparse trail of shredded paper for the pack of "hounds" (us runners) to follow during the run. Where pathways fork, the hare lays down a "false" trail along one of them which the leading hounds will mistakenly follow, and when that trail of paper runs out they have to return to the fork and take the other path, by which time others will already be running on that path and so the lead will have changed. In this way the best runners are handicapped; the aim is not to win, simply to have a good run. I remember a run in West Java near Bandung; the trail passed through villages, all the residents were waving and loving the spectacle, they knew about the run of course, the hare had to get permission for us to run across their fields. I had to jump right over a prostrate cud-chewing buffalo once, got tangled up in a boy's kite string, and towards dusk saw the large brownish flying foxes come out, and had tremendous views across the hills and paddy fields of the open country beyond. Inevitably, one falls somewhere in a slippery section, or must manoeuvre down some steep gully, and ends up quite dirty and dishevelled at the finish line, and later, at one's hotel. There was another run right in the middle of the urban sprawl of Bangkok, which I won't say much about. Suffice it to say, that run finished well inside the red-light district!

We arrived in Pattaya on Friday evening and found a cheap hotel. I had a shower, then met some friends for a meal, delectable Italian cuisine. There were songs, and yarns, and laughter. As time passed the evening grew less structured. We decided to go out and see the town, not that we were completely new to this sort of thing, we had a fair idea of what to expect. Pattaya is a tourist Mecca, full of night life, so dynamic, so vibrant, sometimes overwhelming, with many bars and discos and the like strung out along the streets.

It was a balmy, steamy tropical night. Flying foxes overhead, fireflies flitting everywhere, the sea dead calm except for little wavelets on the beach, and the water filled with teeming millions of little plankton-like crabs and shrimps. Every wavelet and every movement of the crabs and shrimps was accompanied by vivid phosphorescence, so bright you felt able to read by it. The coconuts stood as silent ghosts along the shore, the moon milking down in gentle, sultry splendour, and occasionally the plop of a fish or the clack of a crab, or a silvery flying fish leaving and re-entering the water in a plunge of liquid phosphorescence.

Curiously, the pandemonium across the road didn't seem to clash, this was Asia, youth, and fun, it was there because the beach was there, and in a sense a derivation from it. And so we did a bar crawl, our motto, one bar, one beer. It really was good fun. The bar girls, so many of them, so eager, crowding round, progressively more naked as the night wore on, sitting on our laps, trying to distract us whilst simultaneously frisking us for money – but all in good fun. I must admit that as we had all been away from home for a while we didn't fight them off too hard! I got back to my hotel at 2 am.

On Saturday morning, we went to look for the location of the Hash run. There are always HHH signs in strategic places before a run and we had no trouble finding where the event was to be held, and we arrived there at the scheduled time and signed in for the run. Every run is different, one sees different country and different sights each time, and we were looking forward to this one. We had run for about an hour through rather flat sandy country with a lot of dryland farms and open areas, nearly all of it along established walking tracks and pathways, and we were getting close to the end. In fact, I could see the beer truck not far away, over there at the finish line. To get there, I still had to follow the path around a circuitous route, but the finish line was really quite close at this point.

Now in the Hash it is against the rules to take short cuts; if one does and is found out there is a penalty, a huge mug of beer to drink at one go, and if one fails to finish it, the remaining beer has to be poured over one's head. But as I drew close to the end I could see the finish line not far across the way, and all I had to do to get there was take a short cut across an open field. A sudden sneaky impulse arose inside me, and a nice cold beer beckoned. I had a quick glance around, there was no-one there to see me, so off I shot upon that beckoning short cut. And then something happened that taught me quite a lesson.

As I ran across my short cut ground, feeling smug, suddenly there erupted from just before me a massive swelling cobra, enraged and fully mantled. It must have sensed me there; perhaps it heard my approaching footsteps and objected to my trespass. It shot straight up from deep inside its place, I guess it was a hole, and looked straight into my eyes and frightened me to hell. It seemed to be as tall as me, it was just before my face, and it glared at me with warning, a shocking hostile warning.

It wasn't just that it could kill, but that it seemed to know it, and the deeply alien glitter in its eyes was testimony to it. Never have I looked into the eyes of such hideous, unspeakable, terrible malevolence. Had it struck I would have died, there was no recourse there, in Pattaya. And I had the premonition that it could do with me what it chose, I was utterly at its mercy, and that snake knew it. The impetus of my running was carrying me straight towards it, and I was horrified and frightened past anything you'd dream of. There is something terrible, loathsome and utterly foreign in close communication with a really deadly snake.

And that unblinking, sinister, malignant glare passed into my comprehension, it took about a millisecond, and in that brief moment I absorbed the equivalent of a university degree. Then I took heed and responded with immediate swift alacrity. I put my back legs into gear, and from my gently pacing forward trot I entered straight into a race for the quick reverse sprint of the year, and I backed off from that appalling beast with at least Olympic pace.

I've heard it said that legs go up and down like pistons, but mine were going round extremely fast in direct backward circles. It's also said that fear can cause evacuation of the bowels; well not for me, it was close, I know, but I was too busy running to pause for that. But I tell you true, there's nothing more inclined to put fear into you or loosen your bottom end than to have an angry cobra just six inches from your face. I intensely sensed that snake in my mind, I didn't look around, but I imagined it pursuing me. Back on the track I galloped swiftly to the end, then panting from sheer fright and shock I sank my first beer.

I'll never short-cut Hash again, in case I meet that cobra's mate!

The perils of going to the toilet

No matter where one is there comes a time when one must go to the toilet, and the procedure can be daunting. This time I was again in West Timor. I knew it well, as I had mapped all 14,000 square kilometres of that country for a previous assignment I was on. The members of this current project team were all experienced consultants, they'd seen it all before and knew the ropes. Sometimes we took a neophyte with us to train and mentor, as part of his grooming to be a consultant in his own right. On this particular trip we had such a trainee with us. We were in the field and it was time for lunch, so we pulled over into the shade of a tree in generally scrubby terrain and set about our meal. It was an ideal toilet stop as well and most of us went behind a bush to relieve ourselves.

But the trainee had a greater need, he found a toilet roll and headed for the scrub. Now we were well aware of what goes on in this very dry country, and it was of no more than passing interest to us that a large pig appeared, and grunting amiably, set off in the path of the trainee. I guess we all became aware at once of what was going to happen, for we knew that these pigs are coprophagous (eat faeces), and the benign grunting signalled contentment that an opportunity for lunch may have arrived for the pig as well.

In anticipation of an addition to the learning program of the neophyte, in fact what would probably be a good fast run up the J curve, we waited. Then it happened; with a mighty yell and a great swish of undergrowth the neophyte came bounding from the scrub, pulling up his trousers as he came. Apparently, he didn't twig to what was happening until he heard a grunt, simultaneous with the arrival of the pig's snout. I understand that at the instant this facilitated his ablutions considerably. But reflex is a rapid thing and he was soon in full flight. We feigned surprise, but gee, it was so funny.

In densely populated countries on the other hand it can be difficult to disguise what you are doing when you wish to go to the toilet. It is the practice in some parts of Mumbai (Bombay) for locals, when they want to go, to wade out into the sea, which is usually shallow and calm and placid as a millpond, on the pretext of going for a swim, and squatting down, carry out their ablutions there. But the fish in these waters are well experienced in these habits and are also coprophagous. It is hilarious that these people think that no-one knows what they are doing, when the sea behind them is boiling with these fish.

Habits vary. I had a different experience once in Saudi Arabia when I met a Bedouin Arab whilst walking along a track. We stopped to talk, or try to talk, because language was a problem, and as we were so engaged my friend moved to the side of the track and squatted down upon his haunches. Thinking that this was the custom when talking to a stranger I followed suit and persisted with my halting dialogue. Soon I began to smell an unmistakable smell, and when my friend arose my fears were amply confirmed. Whilst entertaining me, under the cover of his flowing robe, he had been disposing of his excrement!

But walking the plank in Bhutan would take the prize for hazards. Bhutanese people grow two crops, winter wheat, which is mostly brewed to produce Bhutanese "wine", a concoction that varies in strength from beer to that of overproof rum, and summer corn, which is their staple diet. Their houses have three levels, an attic, which is for the storage of food, a central living area, and a lower level where the stock are housed for the winter months. Smoke from the central cooking fire wafts up into the attic where it cures the stored food and keeps rats and other pests at bay, and any household scraps are dropped down below to feed the stock – including human wastes.

If one wishes to go to the toilet in these abodes it is located at the end of a plank, which protrudes from the central living area of the house. This arrangement can be hazardous for the beginner. Filled full of Bhutanese wine one must walk this narrow plank, turn around, perch upon the end of it, all exposed, with pigs, dogs and other nameless beasties down below snorting and baying in anticipation, and perform this vital function. The Bhutanese family are always appreciative that you have made a contribution to the feeding of their stock, but I tell you, it is not for the faint hearted, nor for one who might have had a bit too much Bhutanese wine!

Overnight in Calcutta

It is possible to fly to Calcutta from Bangkok or from Mumbai, which used to be Bombay. This time I flew out of Mumbai. I fly on Air India, and don't try my luck with any of the local airlines. I arrived in Calcutta, departed from the airport and hailed an airport taxi. I have learned that there is only one thing to do in places like Calcutta; I automatically go to the best hotel in town; in this case it was the Oberoi Grand.

When I arrived there, I was met by a suite of fawners, amongst them assorted porters, butlers, receptionists, volunteers, lookers on, lay-abouts, and sundry hotel "staff". I was admitted, automatically of course because I was a foreigner and therefore not only important but undoubtedly rich, and if necessary, someone would be summarily displaced to make room for me.

I was taken to my room. There was Darjeeling tea there, thank God. Darjeeling tea has leaves centimetres across, is served in an old English teapot, and is forever flavourful. The floor was carpeted but marked with the ground-in stains of many spits, where hotel guests had hoiked up their gorge and let it go upon the floor. In these top hotels (and those of the Oberoi chain are famous) the patrons assume that new carpet will be laid next day, because they, mostly Moslems, are wealthy. But it won't, there is no money in Calcutta, so I had to experience their slag.

So, I spent the night. I always set my door; I put my 750 ml aluminium water bottle (empty) behind it at an angle by perching one edge of it upon my pen, such that anyone opening the door would trip it over and the clatter of it falling would alarm me. I keep my travel-bag strap looped underneath one leg of the bed, and my valuables on me or under my pillow.

In the morning I needed a taxi to get to the airport; several airlines fly from there, not only Air India. I went to the hotel checkout people who spoke impeccable English, but as is usual in India they were absolutely in cahoots with their family or relatives and so you get their taxi, no matter what. There is a bus, but one doesn't want the bus. I took one once; it clanked along slowly like a piece of mobile scaffolding, the driver crunching every gear with a long water-pipe gearstick, trundling along in the sticky oppressive heat and human crush of India.

My taxi fronted up at the exit door of the hotel and all hands put my baggage aboard, and all hands wanted to be paid, individually, in multiple US dollars. I told them all to piss off (they speak English, if not the Australian vernacular), then gave a few rupees to a couple of them. Fortunately, these are not violent people.

That dealt with, I surveyed my taxi. Has it got sufficient fuel in the tank? I need to check the gauge, or the driver will put it on me to fill his tank, just a convenient block down the street. Has it got a spare wheel, are the tyres on it serviceable, can the canvas still upon them get me to the airport? Is the boot lid tied down? No-one running along behind? Are there door handles on the inside, where I am, if I want to get out? Are there any other people inside the car? And with the help of the hotel staff we agreed upon the fare, there is no hope of any taxi here having a meter.

So, we set out. He wanted to go down some back road where he told me volubly that he had an injured relative who needed immediate assistance, and I told him no, keep to the main road. Fortunately, I knew the main road. Then he wanted to pick up another passenger; I said no, but I had to be emphatic, just short of hitting him. He cringed. We waited a while beside a bus, disgorging all its foul exhaust fumes straight into my un-closable window. We went on, past a poor man crawling to drink from a broken open sewer. He must drink, or he will die; he will anyway.

We reached the airport. All agreements that were made beforehand at the hotel had then vanished, now he wanted a million US dollars. I collected my bags; I had already worked out how to open the boot. I took up my luggage and began to walk away. He followed, accompanied by an interested retinue, pleading that all his family were starving, also his relatives, back to at least the third generation, not to mention future ones, and all of them were in need of immediate medical aid and nutrition to survive. I walked on. Then I paid him the agreed fare in rupees plus a small tip, and we parted, all satisfied, good friends, proper protocol having been observed.

The airport terminal was crowded. Over in one corner an Indian family was sitting cross-legged on a rug with a big tureen of rice, some dhal and chapattis, having a meal. In the concourse, there were five empty seats more or less together. I walked towards them. As I did so a group of people arrived, led by a fat woman, who was waddling in a pseudo-run towards the vacant seats, large plastic bags of luggage in her hands. She waddled past me and put a bag on each of the vacant seats, thus saving them all for her men. That's Calcutta!

The Great Rift Valley and Addis Ababa

I've seen some curious landscapes around the world but one of them in particular intrigued me. It was a gently sloping plain in Africa, in Ethiopia to be precise, where I was doing a soil survey of a large State Farm called Sheneka. I had arrived in Addis Ababa, and went on down the Great Rift Valley to Sheneka. I came very close to being shot when I first arrived there because the guard was asleep on duty, and so we drove straight on past him. But he awoke, and realizing that he, in turn, could be shot for letting us in un-announced, thought it better to shoot us instead. My driver didn't believe he would, but after he had made one attempt but fortunately hadn't loaded his rifle properly and was shaping up for a second go, I ordered my driver to stop. It took over half an hour and several cigarettes to placate that guard.

I had studied the aerial photographs back in Australia before I departed for Africa and I noticed that the plains in some areas had tiny, white-rimmed, almost perfect circles about five or six millimetres across showing on the photographs, which would be several metres in diameter on the ground, arranged equidistant from each other across that part of the plain. At first, I thought they were due to liquid splashes during processing of the film, but they were too regular and consistent for that.

Sheneka was right on a high edge of the Great Rift Valley, with very deep almost sheer precipices down from it on two sides. It was all volcanic country, and the soils on it were formed on old volcanic ash. On the Farm, I went to one of the spots having these "rings" to investigate, but there was nothing at all to indicate what these little circles might be. There was a lot of prickly pear, from which the locals used to pick and peel the bright pink fruits for sale, but no sign of those circles. I discussed it with some locals, and they began to talk of "rings", mushroom rings! So I located myself very accurately and dug around in the soil, and sure enough I found a fungal mycelium distributed in the form of circles of about the right size. The locals confirmed it. These were old and stable mushroom rings, so definite that they showed up on aerial photographs, if the photographs happened to have been taken at the right time of year. The actual mushrooms – the fruiting bodies – were not present when I was there as it was not the mushroom season. The engineering firm I was working for back in Australia were a bit doubtful though, they thought that the sun might have done my brain a disservice when I told them that I had discovered fairy rings in the middle of Africa!

We had finished our work at Sheneka and were on our way back to town. We camped that night in an isolated thorn enclosure in the bottom of the Rift Valley, about halfway back to Addis Ababa. When we arrived there, we found that a cow had died a little distance from our chosen camp, and all her meat was prey. Hyenas were already there, quarrelling and sparring for their piece of bloody carrion. Hyenas were getting bold in Ethiopia, often hunting in groups, and it was not unknown for them to stalk humans. I once saw a donkey with a hole as big as a soup plate in the back of its thigh where a hyena-sized chunk had been removed. The wound had healed and the donkey was quite mobile, but I certainly didn't want to contribute to a hyena's breakfast. Near Addis Ababa a pair of hyenas stalked me once, they are getting bold there, my guide tried to shoot them but missed, and nearly shot me instead, a quite understandable mistake.

Back in the thorn enclosure, we could see that the air above the dead cow was thick with vultures, soaring down in wide descending circles. Some of them had already landed, bouncing rudely around upon the ground and leaping up onto the carcass, only to be chased off temporarily by the hyenas. The hyenas left when we arrived, but the vultures didn't. They shoved and poked their foul and greedy heads right inside the guts and even up the creature's bottom. They ate a lot of the soft stuff. Then overnight the hyenas returned and finished off the rest, skin, bones and all, leaving just a stain upon the grass. Not a good night for sleeping!

Next morning, we continued on, and soon we came upon a checkpoint. It wasn't there on our way out and it seemed to me to be quite illegitimate, just one of those money-making ventures so common in Africa. The favourite ploy of these bandits is to demand to see your passport whilst waving a gun about and then demand money for its return. They weren't getting mine, I never carry it anyway, I carry a number of expendable photocopies instead. My real passport was always "with the department of immigration getting a visa extension". My colleague was an Ethiopian and he was wise to these happenings, and he told me to say nothing, and leave it all to him. We stopped, got out, and stood beside the car. Then my friend announced, "excuse us just a moment, please, we need to piss". And stupid me, I began to say, "I don't need a piss" but he told me flatly that I did. Beside a bush, feigning it, he said to me out of the corner of his mouth "put your money in your underpants". We did, and then we were searched, but they didn't search our underpants. So on we went.

We arrived in Addis Ababa on a Saturday afternoon, and after some weeks in the bush we were looking forward to some pleasure, food and consolation, and a taste of the bright lights of the city. We needed rest as well but argued that we could always rest tomorrow. There was a place of note, a disused railway station now converted to a disco joint, and it was reputed to be the place to go on Saturday night. It certainly seemed a change from MMBA (miles and miles of bloody Africa). So we washed ourselves, put on clean clothes, and our driver took us there. He was to wait for us in case we didn't like the place and wanted to transfer to somewhere else.

Now, un-attached women are not allowed to enter these places in Africa because they may be prostitutes (for "may be" read "are"). The pros were lining up outside, waiting for single males to roll up who were willing to sponsor their entry, just to get themselves inside. One attached herself to me and another to my mate; we didn't really mind, they seemed nicer people than the ones back at the roadblock in the Rift Valley. Inside we found a table, ordered beer and began to watch the floor show, enjoying this dramatic shift in our circumstances. The pros had gone, the music was fine, very African, and we began relaxing. Then nature called, and I had to find a toilet. I knew not where to go so I asked a waitress, and she pointed to a door in the far wall and said, "Out there". So up I got, went over to the door and opened it, and I was very shocked. I'd walked out into what seemed to be a narrow backyard alley.

There was a small shed up in the top corner, I looked inside, it was atrocious, refuse and excrement all across the seat and floor, full of flies and with a really vivid pong. And then I noticed that all the men were peeing on the fence, and the women were squatting down relieving themselves on the ground at the other end of the yard, they weren't going to use the toilet either. So I joined the men. Then the door burst open, and from it out strode a lithe and agile woman, a tall and proud and lovely young Somali, with no intention to conform. And I tell you true that this is what did happen.

She shunned the squatting women, strode up to the fence, pushed a man aside, took up her skirt, pulled her panties to the side, squared her legs and pissed upon the fence, just like that group of men. Well I tell you what, there was confusion, and general disbelief. All the men forgot themselves and watched her in amazement, and most of them lost full control of what their primary task was and pissed into their boots, or those of neighbours, piss was going everywhere. And then that striking, feline Somali woman stalked calmly back inside, leaving in her wake a trail of male destruction.

When I had collected my wits I also returned inside and went back to my table. I vaguely sensed a sort of squelching, and then I realised that I, or someone else, had pissed in my boots too. Oh, well, have another beer!

Camping out in Timor

There are some areas in Timor that are very like parts of northern Australia. I knew northern Australia very well and could easily recognise the similarities. The reason for it is this. Geologically speaking, Timor is a very young country, with regular pulses of uplift as Australia moves to the north-east and collides ever so slowly with the islands of Indonesia. Timor is in between these two, the meat in the sandwich so to speak, and is being pushed upwards from the sea floor at several millimetres a year, about the same rate as the Himalayas, and most of the landscape is quite steep as a result. The geological materials retain large amounts of salt and carbonates from having been under the sea, and the soils formed on them are greyish in colour and highly alkaline.

However, earth movements due to this collision have been episodic rather than continuous, and there have been times in Timor's distant past when no upwards movement of the land had occurred for quite long periods of time. During these intervals, natural erosion reduced the land to a relatively gentle topography, and the on-going penetration of rainwater down through the soils depleted them of the soluble salts and carbonate residues that were in them. As a result, these soils gradually became less alkaline and eventually slightly acidic, and reddish in colour, quite unusual for Timor. Today some remnants of these flatter areas with reddish soils are still there, and these are the areas that are so similar to parts of northern Australia. One of these areas is north of the township of Soe in mid-West Timor. Like other such remnants, this area has similar native vegetation to those parts of northern Australia, namely a white trunked gum tree (Eucalyptus alba) and kangaroo grass (Themeda species). So close is the similarity that a traveller here could easily imagine that he was in Australia. I knew these areas well and have camped overnight in a couple of them.

On this occasion I had been working through West Timor, camping out whenever decent accommodation in the towns was unavailable. Now it was time to camp again. I had a team of four Indonesians with me whose task it was to assist me, and to learn what they could as we went along. We had eaten in Soe, but there was no place there where we could stay, so we decided to camp in the area of "Australian" country to the north. There were very few people living in this area as the soils were regarded as inferior for agriculture. This suited us perfectly, or it did me, at any rate. To me it was a lovely, gently sloping area with scattered Eucalypts, no people living nearby, no pigs, dogs or cattle, ample privacy, and plenty of space to spread out, just like a piece of northern Australia. We had all the camping equipment we needed, or at least I did, and my assistants told me that they would be OK, they would just sleep in the vehicle.

So I began to pitch my tent. It was a small dome tent with an inner and an outer skin and an inbuilt floor. I had used it previously in the Himalayas, as one of its virtues was that it could be pitched on a hard floor, even indoors if the weather was inclement, or if human fleas were a problem; it did not have to be pegged to the ground. I had taken my tent a little distance from where the vehicle was parked, for privacy. I noticed that my assistants weren't doing anything much, they were just watching me pitch my tent. The job was soon done, and as I stood back to admire my camp, I heard the vehicle's engine start. I wondered, what were they doing? I didn't wonder for very long. They drove forward to just beside my tent and parked right outside my door.

I thought this a bit strange because there was plenty of space and I liked a bit of privacy, but I put it down to their Asian habit of maintaining close company, or perhaps they were concerned about my welfare. However, I had no intention of camping right beside a vehicle containing four snoring Indonesians, so I picked up my tent holus-bolus and moved it onwards about twenty metres. So far so good. But shortly afterwards the vehicle started up again, and they moved it once more to be directly adjacent to the entrance to my tent. It was getting dark by now.

Now I spoke good Indonesian, and I asked in every possible way in English and Indonesian why they were doing this, but nobody seemed to know. The only glimmer of information that eventually emerged was that they were dead scared of the "spirits of the night" and wanted to be as close to my tent as possible, because as a foreigner I was immune from harm by these spirits and they thought that some of that might rub off on them. So we reached a compromise; I left my tent where it was, but turned it around so that the door faced away from their vehicle, and with various threats and imprecations I managed to keep things that way. And so we all retired for the night.

There were two eventful punctuations of that night. The first was when I got up for a pee at a rather dark time of night, and with my torch, I walked towards a clump of trees in a small depression in the ground to relieve myself. As I stood there, half asleep, my eyes grew more accustomed to the darkness, and I dimly saw a faint but strangely regular pattern before me, rather like a jungle camouflage suit. It moved! I turned on my torch, and there right in front of me was the biggest python I have ever seen. The portion I could see seemed to be as thick as my leg, so I quickly concluded my immediate program and hastened back to my tent, closed the entrance door and barricaded it with my clothes. Spirits of the night, was it, that they were frightened of? By then I was frightened, too.

The next episode was when I was awakened by a noise, one I recognised, but for a while I couldn't place. Then I realised what it was; the vehicle's engine was running. My Indonesian friends who were sleeping inside the vehicle had rolled up all the windows to ensure that no "spirits" could get inside and locked the doors. Feeling hot, with so many bodies inside a closed vehicle, they had carefully turned on the ignition and the vehicle's air conditioner to keep them cool, not realizing at first that it wouldn't work unless the engine was running. Then, when that dawned on them, they started up the motor and let it idle on. I arose once more; this wouldn't do, they couldn't sleep inside a closed vehicle or I would find them all suffocated, we were low on fuel, the engine would overheat, and for sure in the morning I would find that the vehicle's battery was flat.

In the middle of the night, with all my crew half asleep and suffering some degree of hypoxia, I had a difficult task before me. It must have been that they were all so much in slumber that I couldn't raise them, but I eventually prevailed and was able to get them to unlock a door; whereupon I turned the air conditioner off, confiscated the vehicle key, rolled down the windows and instructed them to leave things like that. I even offered to stand guard and ensure that no spirits of the night would get at them – not that I was going to honour that promise! And so we all slept on.

Next morning the atmosphere inside the vehicle was palpably foetid and steamy, and the whole ceiling and much of the rest of the interior was dripping with water, the collective condensed breath of my timorous Indonesian staff. Now that morning had come, they were somewhat sheepish and contrite, but all of them were dead keen to be back in Kupang by next nightfall.

I decided not to tell them about the python!

Cocoa, taro and beetles in Rabaul

East New Britain was one of the best Provinces of Papua New Guinea to work in because the "Rascals" hadn't penetrated that far, it was half of an island, and they couldn't get there easily from the mainland. The capital, Rabaul, was a lovely place, situated on the flanks of a semi-dormant volcano that had collapsed after its last big eruption long ago to form a huge marine caldera, with the mountainous old volcanic rim now as a backdrop around to the west. Of course, the recent catastrophic eruption changed all that and commerce and industry re-located to Kerevat, a smaller town with an agricultural research base further to the west, and most of the rest of the population of Rabaul soon went there too.

I was undertaking a soil survey of a large area of cocoa plantations near Pondo on the west coast of the Gazelle Peninsula. The cocoa had been planted underneath coconut trees for shade and shelter, for cocoa cannot take exposure to direct sun or strong wind, and the coconuts provide a second crop. The area included Stockholm, Kuriendahl, Manimbu and Seragi plantations and adjoining areas, all of which were of interest to my client, the New Guinea Islands Produce Company. The existing plantations were old now and the trees senescent and of very low productivity, and my work was to formulate a basis for re-planting the whole area.

When I arrived, I was dropped in between the coconut trees by helicopter and taken by an old Suzuki four-wheel drive to my accommodation in an old house nearby. What I wasn't told was that the Suzuki had no clutch, and as the driver crunched it into gear it jerked away immediately, and I and my bags rolled almost off the tray. I was just saved by one local man, who knew about this thing and grabbed my foot.

At night, from that old house I could see a distant volcano erupting, Mount Ulawun, it was constantly pouring out red lava and emitting dull booms, the forest in the path of the lava was bursting into flame, and although it was on the other side of Open Bay I did wonder at times whether there was any risk that the lava or any of the ejecta would pose a threat to me. But the most amazing thing was the frogs. In the coastal swamps they would croak in unison, a bit raggedly at first but as they croaked, they gradually synchronized their efforts until they were all croaking as one, and then the swamps sounded as though they were populated by just one huge frog with a stupendous, powerful croak. How different from the parrots, which chattered mindlessly at any provocation as they flickered erratically between the trees.

The house I had a room in was occupied by a family group; an ex-Australian, his local wife and their teenage daughter. The husband had become very much a PNG man, he couldn't have lived anywhere else by then anyway. He was keen on rum, didn't trust his wife and abused her verbally at every opportunity, and contrived to spy upon and leer at his daughter when he could. The general standard of housekeeping and cleanliness left a lot to be desired. It was not a happy situation and I contrived to spend as much of my time as possible out in the field on foot, doing my survey work.

Walking in the plantations with my local assistants I was aware of coconuts falling from the canopies above and wondered what would happen if one fell on my head. One man put it very clearly, he said "then you will die". So I stuffed a rag inside my hat, and was very careful to walk between the rows when I could. The fallen nuts were collected for copra by local tribespeople using wooden carts pulled by water buffalo, all at a very slow and shambling pace. In one plantation, I came upon a man and his albino buffalo, which was ambling quietly along under the coconut trees pulling a cart-full of nuts, contentedly chewing his cud as he progressed. When I drew near, although the buffalo could see me and was unperturbed by that, he suddenly perceived my scent, different from that of a local. He lifted his head, looked around wide-eyed, then full of consternation he set out at a brisk trot to get away from me. Then he began to panic and rose to a full gallop, plunging through the plantation, the cart behind him trundling and bouncing, crashing into trees and shedding showers of coconuts at every bound. I thought it politic to retrace my steps a bit and go around that one!

There were always rivers to be crossed, mostly small ones bordered by thick forest, with clear, swiftly flowing water about up to my waist. I could wade them, but even so I took the precaution of having my equipment taken across by my assistants, for they were less likely to be washed off their feet than me. They could also assess the crocodile risk better than I could.

There was another thing I couldn't do also, and that was to walk along the shore on the mangrove roots. There were large mangrove swamps along the coast with abundant exposed but sloping root systems, and in order to traverse them, the locals, with their prehensile bare feet, would simply step from root to root with nimble dexterous ease, gripping with their toes. But with my jungle boots on, as I had to have, I just slipped off these silt-covered roots into the mud. I found it easier to wade through the mire, and that was hazardous because of hidden roots and crabholes. To me, walking on mangrove roots or through the mud between them could not really be classified as "walking" at all. Like so many other ways of "walking" in New Guinea where hands and feet and anything else that can be used to grab with are necessary, it would be more accurately described as "personal quadrupedal semi-desperate perambulatory mode".

Once through the mangroves we came to a turbid tidal inlet where I was to board a dugout canoe for travel further up the coast to Kuriendahl plantation. That was an interesting trip. One of the crew wanted a pee but was strangely reluctant to pee over the side because I was there. It wasn't that he was worried about exposure, nor was I, it was that he thought that I mightn't appreciate the smell! The men laughed and sang as they paddled in beautifully clear water speckled with brilliantly coloured little fishes. But when we came to areas of dark, deep water silence would suddenly prevail, and they would all paddle strongly and swiftly until the canoe was back in shallow water again. Why, I do not know, but I suspect that there were real or mythical creatures of the deep that they would rather not have any truck with.

At Kuriendahl we beached the canoe, and sitting there on a washed-up log at the edge of the forest was the tribal leader of that place, in full ceremonial dress (head-dress, arse grass and a full complement of weapons) with the most venomous and menacing scowl I have ever seen on a human face, waiting for us. Somehow, he knew that we were coming. It was most intimidating, but my assistant eventually left the canoe and with great deference went to ask permission from this terrible spectre for us to work upon his land. At first, he was loud, aggressive and imperious, but I think that was just a formality, because he very quickly shed his hideous unwelcoming cloak and became quite friendly. He took us to his village nearby, almost crowing to his subjects with his importance at being visited by a white man. After due formalities we left him and set off down a narrow track far into the forest. At one lonely spot with something akin to magic, smacking of witchcraft, and completely soundlessly, he suddenly materialized from the bush beside our track. He must have been watching us, from within the adjacent forest!

The work done, it was time to return to Rabaul. A helicopter had come for me, a Hughes 500E with five blades on the rotor, and down between the coconuts it came to pick me up. The pilot clearly wasn't going to actually land, but as he hovered the door opened, and I saw to my surprise that the helicopter was already full of people, and there seemed to be no place for me to sit. Undeterred, I thrust my soil auger inside, unfortunately into one poor fellow's ear, and scrambled aboard as best I could. We emerged from the coconuts, and the pilot landed in a clearing a short distance further on where we could re-arrange ourselves. I found out then that the fellow who received my soil auger in his ear was the PNG High Commissioner to Australia. He didn't seem to mind, it was probably par for the course for him whilst he was back in New Guinea. The other people on board were government sightseers from Rabaul accompanying the dignitary, after all it was a free trip for them, so they just filled the helicopter up without a single thought as to where I and my equipment might fit.

That night I called in at a social club, I think it was the Golf Club. There were some wild white men resident in Rabaul who'd been in PNG for most of their life. One of them was a regular at the Club, and always sat out on the back veranda. At dusk the giant staghorn beetles, the three-inch-long ones with two horns, pests of the coconut palms and plentiful in number, would fly into the light with a deep loud droning sound. They would crash-land upon one's arms and legs and cling there with the claws and spikes upon their legs, often drawing blood. But this miscreant could deal with them, he welcomed them, in fact that's why he sat out there at the back. The beetles landed on him several at a time, clawing at his skin. He'd grab them, one by one or two at a time, pull off their wings, legs and head, and stuff them into his mouth and eat them, with a slurp of beer. Curious, I asked him, "do they taste good?". He said "yes, delicious! And I don't have to pay for my grub". I went inside and ordered steak and chips, but I found that after the staghorn beetle performance I wasn't really in the mood for a meal.

I had a request from Harry Chan, the then Prime Minister of Papua New Guinea, to go with him to his property in New Ireland, an island in the east of the country, and give him some advice on his land, gratis, of course. We flew over there in his Bell Long Ranger helicopter, a spectacular flight through the central mountains of New Ireland to his farm on the north coast. Then he and his wife gave me lunch, and a vehicle to look around with. New Ireland is a lovely place with beautiful beaches, more like those of the Pacific islands than those of the PNG mainland. He had some very good soil for cocoa there, with dark, highly organic topsoils for the shallow feeder roots and a deep substrate for the central tap root, for although cocoa is a shallow-rooted feeder it needs to be well anchored in the soil or it will blow over; it is usually grown under a cover of coconut trees for this reason. The workers in the plantations there carry a lump of boiled taro in their sarong for food, and periodically they bite off a chunk of this dense, dismal tuber with teeth like bolt cutters and chew it to quell their hunger.

The accuracy with which these local people can navigate through lowland forest is amazing. There are no aspect differences at all at such latitudes, no moss on one side of the tree trunks, no shadow to one side, in fact there seemed to be no evidence at all on the forest floor of any differences between north, south, east or west. The sun was directly overhead as these were the equatorial tropics, but because of the closed forest canopy above, little sunlight penetrated to the forest floor. I had asked a small band of people to take me to an old building, a derelict house on the north coast that I had marked on my aerial photographs.

On our way we passed an old abandoned village site, with a brilliant flowering Poinciana tree and a grove of coconuts, sure signs of an old village. Without hesitation two men climbed the trees and threw the coconuts down to us. The nuts had been warming in the sun but the milk inside them was deliciously cool and slightly effervescent. After drinking the coconut milk, we cut a slice off the outer green husk of the nuts with a machete, which because of its curvature, fitted beautifully inside the shell of the nut and formed an ideal spoon for scooping out the soft gelatinous young flesh. We continued on to the coast, and emerged from the forest onto the coastal dune and sandy beach right beside the old building that I had asked them to take me to. I had secretly kept a compass on them the whole time and never once did they deviate from the correct course. It was uncanny; they were real forest bushmen.

There was one very pleasant village located on a broad sand dune just beside the beach, under a shady cover of whispering coconut palms. The houses were elevated as most are in PNG, with roofs of palm fronds or thatched with kunai grass, and had well-made wooden verandas.

This was a very peaceful village and most of the inhabitants didn't wear very much in the way of clothes. There was one woman in the happy group that came to meet me who arrested my attention. She was topless, as all the women were, but she had two very different breasts. One was quite pendulous, hanging almost to her waist, as most of them are, but the other one was as pert and shapely as one of Marilyn Munroe's. I conjectured that one of them (the pert one) was used to rear her children, and the other (the pendulous one) was for suckling baby pigs. She also had different eyes, one was dark brown as is usual in PNG and the other was bright blue. Don't ask me which eye matched which breast! Maybe she was just born that way.

Landing at Mount Hagen

I spent some time working in the Sandaun Province of Papua New Guinea, based in Vanimo but mostly working out of Aitape. I had to go to Port Moresby at times and I used to catch the New Guinea Airlines Fokker Friendship in Wewak; I twice met former prime minister Michael Somare on the flight. Once when we were almost at touchdown in Moresby the pilot realized he was on the wrong approach and suddenly did a very steep bank to the left, levelled out and almost immediately landed on the correct strip, no fuss, just normal PNG. Sometimes it would be on a Twin Otter out of Vanimo or Aitape. All flights landed at Mount Hagen on the way.

But at other times I had to go in a single engine light aircraft, smaller than a Twin Otter, and on this occasion, with an Australian pilot, we took off from Aitape. It was the wet season, and from Aitape onwards the highlands were blanketed in cloud, dark and forbidding, no lightning though. We flew up towards Hagen through the clouds, it was pretty rough, but acceptable enough given the time of year. The pilot knew when he was over Hagen, but it was completely shrouded in cloud and he had to see the place before he could land, so he just circled overhead for a while, waiting. Then a hole opened in the cloud and a shaft of sunshine shone down through it, and we could see the forest below. The pilot didn't muck about. He quickly lined up with the hole, put his aircraft into a steep dive, and shot straight down through the void, on full power, airframe shuddering. It seemed very precarious, it was too fast and steep to be rough or to realize what was happening, but very quickly we were beneath the cloud and shooting along right above the trees, and we could see the strip. He landed normally, except for a massive spray of water from the wheels. The pilot and passengers thought nothing of it, it was common practice in the wet season, and it worked quite well. But by the living saviour, one had to hold on, not just to one's seat but one's stomach contents as well. One of those PNG experiences where you have to get used to it and trust the pilot. Just another landing that sorely taxed my continence!

A military coup in Ethiopia

I was back in Ethiopia, based in Addis Ababa, on a natural resource management project. I was getting near the end of my assignment, and in the process of planning my return to Australia. I had walked about half a city block from my work office in a multi-story building down to the Ethiopian Airlines agency and was confirming my flight details when it happened.

It began some distance up the street, seventy or eighty metres away, outside the Ministry of Defence. I was in the thick of the initial action. Two tanks and a truckload of troops drew up at the Ministry gate and demanded entry, rifles ready, intent upon a coup. I learned later that they were one of Colonel Mengistu's advance assault squads. The guards refused them entry and raised their guns, and then all hell broke loose. There began a hail of bullets from high-powered automatic rifles that rattled up and down the streets, and all the people started to run. The residents of that city had seen it all before, they melted instantly away into the side alleys, and completely vacated the streets.

Inside the airline office I had no escape. Bullets were whizzing down the street and smacking into the building I was in, a long, sustained hail of them, and all I had for shelter was a half metre wide concrete column. As I hid behind that pillar the windows of the office were smashed, glass was everywhere, and bullets zapped past and ricocheted around the room. It was half an hour at least before I could slither to the floor and make my way, with guidance from the staff, who were down behind the counter and wanting out as well, to a small back door that opened onto an alley that led back towards my office. I bolted down the alley, there were no people anywhere by this time, they had all gone home to hunker down and wait it out. This was quite new to me, but they had done it all before, time and time again. My work office had been completely vacated except for one person, my driver; he knew where I had gone because he had earlier offered to drive me there and had waited in the office for my return, and frightened as he was, that loyal and committed man was there to drive me home.

By now the streets were filling up with troops and armoured personnel carriers. We set out in our white Toyota Land Cruiser wagon through the abandoned city, sneaking around the military. On our way to the housing unit I was living in, which was on the road to the airport, we had to cross a large and now completely vacant square. I knew it well, it had red flags on all the corners and communistic slogans everywhere. There was no clear road, you had to just drive across it, and so we entered at one end and proceeded diagonally across the square to get onto the road that led out to the airport. We were almost in the centre of the square when with consternation I saw that tanks and truckloads of troops were pouring into the square from the other side. We were the sole civilian traffic.

Then something quite arresting happened. One tank pulled out of line, and its driver slid his tank towards us. He stopped his tank and lowered down and aimed his gun straight at us, and swinging the turret around, he followed us with his gun as we progressed across that square. I told my driver, do not panic, just go slow, and not really knowing what to do I wound my window down and put my head in full view so that the tank driver could see that I was a foreigner, and therefore no threat to him or the coup. And with his telescopic sights he seemed to get the message, he did not fire. I would have died for sure if he had, but thanks to my driver I survived, and soon got back to my accommodation.

I shared my residential unit with a colleague, a pom, and as poms do, he had reached it first. We took stock and wondered what our options were now. Then we heard a noise, a dull, distant roaring sound. My colleague stood upon the toilet seat and looked out the small window up there and said "Bai jove!" I climbed up beside him and looked out, and uttered the Australian equivalent. There was a roiling cloud of black smoke and an almighty racket, it was Ethiopia's ancient worn out tanks going out to secure the airport. They came down the road three abreast, running over footpaths and centre strips, ripping up the road and all beside it with their tracks, intent only upon getting to the airport in a hurry. And it seemed that nothing short of failed mechanicals, which seemed quite likely, or running out of fuel, which also seemed likely, would deter them.

I lay upon the floor of my flat for three days, with helicopter gunships manoeuvring overhead and tanks and troops firing up and down the road outside. We had no food except half a loaf of stale bread and a gumboot full of avocados, but we did have water. There was no local information at all on the progress of the coup, but we had reports from London on my short-wave radio advising all poms to stay indoors, and giving some information as to what was happening. And whilst I was lying there upon the floor I wrote up my Report, why not, I had to do it sometime, and there was nothing else to do anyway.

Then, after those three days, pack donkeys and their drivers came back in and proceeded down the road as though nothing had happened, so with the transport system returning to normal I could cautiously venture forth again and buy some bread and pineapples. The pineapples were fresh, but my English friend thought there was something wrong with them, because in England the only pineapples he had eaten had glazed translucent flesh and of course were clearly past their prime.

Next day our driver came for us, and looking and feeling pretty scruffy we ventured back to our work office, where I handed in my hand-written Report. We went downtown for lunch and entered a calm but tense and wary city. The tanks were parked on corners now, mostly on the aprons of service stations, their crews nearby, alert for any trouble. We met some friends who had been staying at one of the main hotels in town, and they described for us what they had seen of the action within the city area. Apparently one tank lost control going down a steep section of road and shot right through the safety fence at the bottom, down a precipice, and straight into the rear garden of the hotel. Undeterred, the driver drove his tank back and forth inside the hotel garden looking for a way out, right over concrete seats and shelters but meticulously avoiding all the flower beds, before finally giving it away and exiting through a hedge on the other side.

The airport had been re-opened, but my original flight schedule was of course in tatters. I managed to secure a seat to Abu Dhabi on a flight scheduled to leave quite soon. From there I was able to get on a flight to Mumbai, then across India to Madras, and hence with Garuda to Singapore. We flew at night along the line of oil wells with their flaming gas pipes to the north of Sumatra and on to Singapore at dawn, and did a turn around it. Singapore has always been one of my favourite cities and in the early morning light it looked quite beautiful. We landed in a completely different world.

In Singapore, one of the cleanest and most disciplined cities in the world, I hadn't formed any further plans, I was just relieved to be free again. I left the airport, went into the city, and bought a kilogram of rambutan. I sat down on a bench beside a rubbish bin and watched, slack-jawed and wondering, as the population of that clean, busy, stable and civilized city passed before me. I ate my rambutan, carefully putting the skins and seeds into the bin. You don't drop litter in Singapore.

I was quite unwashed, I hadn't shaved all week nor changed my clothes, and as I sat, fearful every minute to be charged with vagrancy and having no fixed address, I wondered if some passer-by might throw me down a coin.

Insurgents, militias and human hazards

Travel in countries such as Cambodia, Myanmar, Angola, Mindanao, Somalia, Yemen and others is always fraught with danger of some sort. There is the ever present one of being kidnapped and held for ransom, especially within the major cities and in the more remote parts of these countries. Cambodia is just across the Mekong River from Vietnam and there is a bridge across the river just to the south of Phnom Penh, which is not far from Saigon. Stealing of vehicles is very common in Phnom Penh. Unless any new or almost new vehicle is securely locked up at night it is almost certain to be stolen and taken across to Vietnam for sale. Many of the international peace-keeping force vehicles were taken, as they were essentially un-owned and left out in the open at night. But it's not only at night, people are held up at gunpoint on the highways away from Phnom Penh and have their vehicle forcibly taken from them, motorcycles too, any resistance and the driver would be shot; a bullet is a cheap price for them to pay for a vehicle, and there is very little likelihood of repercussion.

After the Vietnam war there were many unexploded land mines and many legless survivors of the ones that did go off, who were left unable to work and had no income, and there was no welfare organization or restitution of any sort to assist them. The solution for many was blatant highway robbery. These victims would collect at bridges and other road constrictions and flag down passing vehicles and demand money. Most locals sympathized with them and willingly gave them money, in fact it was seen as antisocial not to do so; passing vehicles would just slow down and hand some cash through the vehicle window or toss it on the ground beside them.

I saw a land mine go off one day. Usually, being aware of the danger, I would only walk across ground that had been cultivated or thoroughly trampled by cattle, so that any mines would have been exploded long ago. In Vietnam and Cambodia all forested areas near the notorious 17th parallel had skull and crossbones signs warning of the danger, and no-one ever ventured in there. But one time in Vietnam a mine did go off not far from me, near a paddy field where women were planting rice. There was a thud and a "whoosh!" and a column of mud and water erupted about ten metres into the air, but there was no visible activity or concern, it may have been an everyday occurrence. At the time, I was jokingly helping the women plant rice, to their huge amusement. I borrowed a coolie type hat and took a handful of seedlings and industriously stuck each plant into the mud, trying my best to keep a straight line. No-one else worked – they all just watched me, and laughed at my ineptitude. They would have laughed about that for weeks – a white man, planting rice! Woman's work!

Somalia, Djibouti, Eritrea and Yemen line both sides of the Gulf of Aden and the Red Sea, which converge at a stricture off Djibouti, a very busy shipping lane connecting the Indian Ocean with the Mediterranean Sea and leading into the Suez Canal, cutting off the long and arduous sea journey around the Cape of Good Hope and along the west coast of Africa. These countries do not have the capacity to blockade the Gulf due to rigorous international supervision of those waters, but they can and do undertake piracy at sea, not only for blatant theft but hostage taking as well. Somalia does not maintain an adequate border patrol, arguing that a summary bullet is far cheaper than the wages of a border guard. Mogadishu is one of the most dangerous and pathetic cities in the world. A similar situation exists in the Persian Gulf, where Iran is positioned to control the narrow shipping channel of the Strait of Hormuz, and Oman is not far to the south.

From the eastern reach of the Mediterranean Sea there are Syria, Iraq, Iran, and Afghanistan in an easterly line, all Moslem countries that have been problematic for travellers and are increasingly more so. Turkey, the turn-point to the north, could go either way. That bloc, if it were to include

Egypt, Saudi Arabia and the Emirates, could form an alliance as potent as that of Europe. These are dangerous countries. Inexperienced travel in these countries is a no-no.

The danger in New Guinea from rascals is very real. They come alive by night and sneak into the cities, stealing and looting wherever they can, with no regard for human life. They hadn't yet penetrated to the far north-west in Sandaun Province when I worked there, nor to the Gazelle Peninsula (Rabaul) because of the cost of transport from the mainland. I was in my room in a hotel beside the airport in Port Moresby one night when quite unbeknownst to me a bunch of them came into the restaurant when the guests were having their evening meal and robbed them all at gunpoint, then vanished into the night. One doesn't use public transport in Moresby, because in the buses one is quite likely to be stabbed by a machete rammed through the rear of the seat. The rascals will even prey upon their own kind. I heard about a schoolgirl riding her bicycle to school near Wewak who was grabbed, raped, and had her school lunch stolen, then she was just thrown into the roadside bushes. Justice in New Guinea still runs mostly on tribal grounds, one's tribal affiliation is far more important to them than the "law". There is a lot of petty theft and crime, even in the government-run Post Offices. If one buys a stamp one has to stand and watch after purchase to make sure that the stamp is actually affixed to the envelope and the envelope is posted, or the employee will pocket the money, or open and trash your mail and steal the stamp. Be careful driving over bridges in country areas. The locals often resent this access and place spikes sticking up between the longitudinal wooden planks to puncture tyres, so as a precaution one always drives on the cross planks to the side.

The Moslem Provinces of the Philippines are also dangerous. One time in the Province of Cotobato I was late getting back to my well-guarded hotel, anyone at all coming over the fence there at night would immediately be shot by the proprietor, no questions asked. As I travelled homewards darkness fell, all road and field traffic ceased, and no dwelling showed any lights. It was a bit unnerving, but nothing untoward happened. In another Moslem Province, Marawi, I had to travel down a narrow road notorious for its roadblocks and hostage taking. As in all such circumstances I hired an old-model nondescript vehicle that no-one would want to steal, with air-conditioning and tinted windows so that I could not be seen inside, and had the driver vetted very thoroughly. He was given clear instructions that in the event of any rebel roadblock he was to reverse back the way we had come, fast. The rebels were easy to distinguish from regular soldiers by their boots – the military wore proper government issue boots, but the rebels wore anything, sandshoes, thongs, even bare feet.

In any Moslem country things can go wrong very quickly. In Indonesia, a normally benign country, in densely populated areas when the mid-day hour of worship approached, I would stop work and go to the nearest village, sit down on a bench in full public view and do nothing, and stay there for an hour or so. I couldn't attend the prayer meeting of course, nor did I want to, but that was accepted as suitably deferent to the religious matters of the moment. In one country area, I nearly got chopped up with machetes and chunkals (hoes). I had been searching for a relatively undisturbed area to assess, hopefully with some remnant native vegetation, and I found one. So I got in there with my soil auger and equipment and started to bore a soil inspection hole. Then the fields around erupted, and local workers began to run towards me, brandishing all sorts of fearsome weapons. It was only then that I realised that this area was so untouched because it was a burial ground, a cemetery. I raced for my vehicle and we got out of there very quickly.

Travelling through a village in West Java one day we accidentally bumped a teenage girl. We were going very slowly, aware of the hazard, but this girl wasn't looking where she was going and ran straight into the side of our vehicle. She was quite unhurt, but knowing the potential for retribution we didn't even think of stopping, we shot out of that village fast. Our plan was to go straight to a police station and wait it out. But along the way a motorcycle passed us, he was clearly going to warn the next village of our misdemeanour and ask them to stop us. We deviated and took a different route.

Almost shipwrecked off Sumbawa

I was working on a project on the island of Sumbawa in Indonesia. Part of the project was to assess the potential for use of vacant land around the Tambora volcano, now thought to be extinct, with a view to resettling people there from the densely populated island of Java. The main object of the trip was to assess the land and water resources around the Tambora peninsula, and in particular any watercourses that seemed to have promising potential for irrigation.

Initially, we were based at Raba (Bima). From there we hired a local passenger ferry to cruise along the eastern side of Tambora to see what we could of the land, because there were no roads there. We landed only once, and were taken ashore by enthusiastic locals in a canoe, whom I amused by helping to paddle with my soil auger! This journey was fairly unsuccessful, so we boarded a plane to return to Mataram on the island of Lombok, a route that at first took us along the east side of Tambora. Then we did a very naughty thing, we effectively hijacked the plane! The pilot was a laid-back sort of guy and quite readily accepted our request, which was to fly low along the shoreline of our survey area so that we could get a good look at it. The other passengers must have wondered why we were flying so low and so slowly!

For the next part of our survey we moved to a logging camp on the northern tip of the Tambora peninsula to investigate the forest there, which had regrown after the eruption of Tambora in 1815, a very powerful eruption that destroyed the forest, which had by then substantially regrown. Underneath the one to two metres of volcanic ash human artefacts such as knives and horseshoes were still being found. From there we could see Satonda Island offshore, a new volcano, and at night the many fishing boats at sea using lights to attract fish, to later dry on land.

After that, we still had one job to do. We needed to check out a stream arising on the north-eastern side of the mountain to see if it held permanent water, and showed any prospects for irrigation of crops such as vanilla. We drove down the west coast and across the neck of the volcano to Sanggar on the eastern coastline, which was as far as we could go by vehicle. Needing breakfast, we asked around for someone to climb a coconut tree and throw us down some nuts, but there wasn't a tree-climber to be found ('tidak ada yang naik', in Indonesian), so we breakfasted on bananas (pisang).

With help from our guide we managed to procure a boat with a 20-horsepower outboard motor. The boat was small, and the sea was rough, so after some discussion most of the survey team returned to Mataram, and I and one other, Danny, stayed to complete the job. Little did we know then that the outboard motor was temperamental, and was to nearly cost us our lives. We boarded; there were the two of us, plus some Indonesian locals who knew the area we were going to visit. The engine only stopped a couple of times and was successfully restarted, but it was an ill-omen. We eventually arrived at a secluded cove and disembarked, we were told that we couldn't go all the way to the stream we were interested in immediately, because the sea there was too rough during the day, and we needed to wait until just before dawn to attempt a landing there.

So we settled down for the night, and waited for the sea to subside. We had a good fire going and baked some bananas in the coals, cooking ones, that tasted a bit like banana flavoured potatoes, very nice. Just before dawn we awoke, the sea was miraculously calm, and our friends were actively preparing for the journey ahead of us. We set out on a dead calm sea, marveling at the difference from yesterday. But our joy was to be short-lived, for when we arrived offshore there were huge waves breaking on the beach and it was far too rough, a boat landing was impossible. Danny and I reckoned we could swim ashore, but there was no way we could have gotten back to the boat. So we returned to our sheltered cove, and decided to walk to our stream instead, as it was still quite early in the day.

Then there were preparations! Danny and I took just a water bottle each, but our escorts did a lot more. They strapped their rubber thongs to their feet with twine and began to eat raw eggs, to give them strength, they said; more like courage, I thought. We wondered, speculated, what we were letting ourselves in for, was there something we didn't know? We soon found out. At first, we walked along the beach, and although the tide was low, just around the corner the sea completely covered the sand, right up to the cliffs behind. Then it all became clear, we had to wade through the waves along that part of the coast; the twine stopped their thongs from being washed away, and the raw eggs gave them bravado, if not courage.

We arrived at our stream, it was really quite close. There were several Indonesians there, they had been collecting white honey (madu putih) from the upper slopes of the mountain, and were busy dismembering deer for venison. We all spoke Indonesian so there were no communication problems. White honey is not really white but translucent, and very, very sweet, prized by local folk, grubs and all, served in any old bottle, with a rag or grass stopper. They gave us some venison, it was delicious. Our stream was a beauty. It was about four metres across and a metre deep, and flowing very swiftly. The hunters told us it was like that all year round, so we had all the information we needed. So now, we had to return to our camp. On the way back I wanted to run, and Danny obliged, but he was a bit of an alternative type and had rather pointy shoes with a heel, and soon got sore feet.

At camp, the boat had arrived to take us back to Sanggar, and as it was still morning, we all quickly climbed aboard and set off. This was where our trip became interesting. The sea was quite rough and soon the locals became seasick, and applied to me for medicine (obat sakit) to cure it. I had nothing specific for motion sickness so administered aspirin, and the placebo effect kicked in and all soon felt well again. And then the motor stopped. Once was OK, it restarted, but then it quit again and just could not be restarted. We were opposite a sheer cliff with waves pounding against it, a lee shore, and we were drifting inexorably towards it. There was no panic, but I for one was anxiously scanning the cliffs for a way up! Only about 50 metres from where the waves were beating against the cliffs, and very close to being shipwrecked, the damned engine restarted, and thankfully, kept going all the rest of the way. Back on dry land, there was still no tree climber, but those bananas sure tasted good!

Some months later, by chance, I met Danny again in the Edsa Plaza Hotel in Manila, a glad reunion; he rushed impetuously to hug me, but quickly changed his hug for a less intimate handshake! We re-lived Tambora, but with no raw eggs, and we didn't have to tie on our thongs!

Strip-lines, tropical forest and mangroves

Don't believe anyone who tells you in rapturous tones about the beauty and pleasure of being in a tropical forest. All such people whom I have met hadn't really been in one, they had just read some travelogues or been in a national park or two. I have worked in these forests and I can tell you that they aren't anyplace you would really desire to be. The highlight of working in these places is invariably the same, finishing the job and getting out again. One such job I did was in the foothills of the Highlands of Papua New Guinea.

For the main part of the work I used "striplines", which were just straight lines surveyed through the bush with enough of the undergrowth slashed by machete to be able to see and walk along the line, at least for a week or two until the forest re-grew and reclaimed the space. I had employed a local surveyor from Port Moresby with not much more than a theodolite to his name to carry out the work. It was a good arrangement because he understood the local labourers and kept a tally of their hours worked and paid them whatever was their due every week.

He also seemed to know when a new tribal boundary was coming up, which was important because men from one tribe must not work uninvited on land belonging to another tribe. At the new boundary, he would pay off all the existing staff and re-employ new ones from the new tribal community, train them in their work, and carry on. They used the "stick over stick" method of progression, which meant that a sharpened stick was placed every 100 metres or so in line with previous sticks, and by sighting over each stick with the theodolite they moved progressively onwards. It wasn't very accurate, but I carried a GPS (global positioning system) so that at intervals along the lines I could find out exactly where I was.

My surveyor was a good worker, but he blotted his record by falling in love with a woman from a tribe located on the banks of the Pual River ("hap i kam Pual" or "half he come Pual") which meant the land on our side of the river. The other side was "hap i go Pual". I'm not sure who seduced who, but he wanted to take this woman back to Moresby with him. The only way back for him was to fly, because there were hostile tribes everywhere if he was to travel overland, but his Company would not pay an extra fare for his woman, and she couldn't have gone overland on her own. I'm not sure how it worked out in the end, but I am sure he would have been better off without her, she just wanted a free trip to Port Moresby.

For those people who think of tropical forests as some sort of paradise and whose only experience of it has been a gravelled tourist walkway to some vantage point or piece of forest (e.g. the Curtain Fig Tree) let me put a few things straight for you. People who expound the "pleasantness'" of the "tropical jungle" just don't know what they're talking about. It's as hot as hell under that canopy, and so thickly humid that one sweats constantly, even standing still. But if you stand still for even a moment leeches loop up over your boots and get inside them, and the first thing you know about it is the squelching feel of blood saturating your socks. At every spot you stop to work mosquitoes accumulate in clouds, big voracious buggers, and they take no notice whatsoever of repellents, and there are crocodiles in every waterhole and swamp. Across your path are always rotten logs, some of them two metres thick, they look sound enough until you start climbing over them, whereupon the outer shell gives way and you are precipitated into a rotting mass of pulped wood and caterpillar-sized wriggling grubs, big grey things in their millions, they come all over you and get inside your clothing. It is also very easy to trip and fall, but the stripline floor is speckled with the razor-sharp remains of cut shrubs and saplings, all pointing up towards you, and to fall on one would be calamitous. And just for fun, at intervals one has an unexpected sudden descent into half a metre or so of slimy mud which you just can't see from on top – but they can. Did I do all those university degrees to spend my time like this?

And then there are the log bridges, the bain of my life. I have crossed many log bridges, some only a few centimetres wide. I had to wear jungle boots (Malaysian of course) and I frequently slipped and fell off those bloody log bridges into the slimy green fluid down below, and that's not really good fun. The natives go barefoot and are quite prehensile, agile, and aware, and they also have an innate sense of balance, way beyond mine. but my feet weren't like theirs, I wore slippery wet jungle boots. They, recognizing my inability, always left me a sapling "staff" about 5-8 cm thick to balance with as I crossed the log bridge. Those New Guinea people are to be recognized though, they are always kind and considerate, they cared for me, even if they saw me as something of an idiot in their own terms.

One fallen tree we had to cross was over a metre thick but so rotten it had a dense growth of grass on it and looked just like a dam wall. It creaked alarmingly when stood upon, and it didn't help that down in the water beside it a large crocodile was visible, seemingly lying in wait. I was offered a piece of sage advice concerning weak log bridges – my guide said, "don't put all your weight on it". I dined out on that one for quite a while until I discovered that it actually works! You start out standing tall, walk swiftly, and as you cross the bridge you progressively lower your body height until at the other end you are crouching low. Whether it worked or not, that procedure was all I needed to ensure that I fell off the thing. Thankfully, it rains about half the time which dilutes the mud and slime and blood, and soothes the leech and mosquito bites that cover half one's body.

Getting lost was a bit of a problem too, for I was often travelling through the forest on my own. There was one place in very dissected country where I could not cross a gully where my staff had done because the log bridge they had left for me was far too narrow and bouncy, my jungle boots would have slipped on it, and I would have suffered yet another dunking. So I carefully marked my location and moved off downstream until I found a place to cross, and then walked back to the strip-line. From that spot, at the other end of the log bridge, directly opposite the exact tree I had been at and marked before, I looked around very carefully but could not see the strip-line, neither back the way I had come nor in front. I knew better than to panic. I could not retrace my footprints in the litter of the forest floor, and it took me half an hour of diligent searching from that marked position until things finally came into focus and I could see along the line. What a relief!

Once, another time, at the start of a stripline, I was attacked by a wild pig. Fortunately, I had my vehicle close at hand. Finding the start of the stripline after only a week wasn't easy, the regrowth comes back fast in Sandaun Province. It began in an old cocoa plantation with lovely ripe pods still around, and I munched the delicious pulp around the young beans along the way. I was a short distance off-road inspecting the landscape as part of my soil survey work when I came across a large forest tree of a sort I knew, and I was collecting and eating its fallen lychee-like fruits when

I was accosted by a pig, who obviously thought that all the fallen fruit belonged to him. Without hesitation, he charged, and I just made it into my vehicle. Then, all the way back to the "road" he charged at the vehicle's wheels, tusking the tyres, sliding off into the ditch, and coming again, giving the vehicle a sizeable thump with each impact. He never left off until we reached the road.

The other thing one learns is that travel through mangroves is difficult. The trees grow closely together and have abundant sloping roots which are exposed above the shoreline mud at low tide, and in tropical countries the local people take advantage of these roots to travel around the coast. They hold onto the tree stems and step from root to root, clinging on with their toes. These roots are slippery and difficult to "walk" on if one is wearing jungle boots, so it is unpleasant but safer for us to just wade through the mud and tolerate a couple of falls, in truth, not a good way of going. It's OK for the locals, they have very nimble feet. Of the plant as a whole, there are more of these roots under the mud than the whole top of the canopy. The mud harbors abundant life including the well-known mud crabs, and hosts the little reproductive pneumatophores (mangrove seedlings) which float out of the mud at high tide and travel across the sea.

Much of the coastline of the Northern Territory is lined with mangroves. Mangroves grow around the world and there are many species, even one that grows in fresh water in Australia's north (Barringtonia spp.). Mangroves are not very tall, but they have a dense overlapping canopy and so qualify as low forests. They form an important marine ecosystem, supporting many sorts of fish, adults and their fry, and many crabs, including the famed mud crab. They also create still water which causes sediment from rivers to settle out, and they protect the shore from wave erosion. If one is unfamiliar with them, one's first few forays into mangroves provide an interesting experience. They are full of tiny sand flies, more correctly called biting midges, and they swarm all over every exposed part of the body and deliver their tiny but multiple bites. These are just as annoying as mosquito bites, but the worst is still to come. After a few hours, the bites become red and swollen and very itchy and one is compelled to scratch, which is the worst way to treat them as they can be scratched raw. A mild immunity seems to develop after a few such exposures.

A severe episode of mangrove dieback struck Australia's Gulf of Carpentaria in the summer of 2015-16 affecting 1,000 kilometres of coastline between the Roper River in the Northern Territory and Karumba (near Normanton) in Queensland. Losses were most severe in the NT, where around 5,500ha of mangroves suffered dieback. The Robinson and McArthur River coastlines lost up to a quarter of their mangroves. This happened at the end of an unusually long period of severe drought conditions, when coincidentally, sea levels in the western Pacific dropped by up to 20 centimetres, so that the mangroves suffered severe moisture stress. They appear to have died of thirst.

There are few areas of tropical forest in the Northern Territory, but they are abundant in north Queensland. Areas of thick tall forest occur in the north east of Arnhem Land around Gove where the rainfall is higher and more spread out across the seasons, and they are the Territory's closest approximation. There are, however, some areas of an ancient forest tree, Allosyncarpia ternata. These are remnants of a formerly much more widespread tropical forest, now reduced by a drier climate and fire to a few sheltered and wetter ravines. The best one is in the Jim-Jim falls gorge.

Perhaps the most uncomfortable place in the tropics is Pontianak in Kalimantan, which is just a wide sea of mud and mangroves in almost flat land, right on the equator. You cannot see the sea, it's very hot and humid, there's warm rain, and it's lousy with voracious sand flies, mosquitoes and leeches. And the people? They used to eat people.

My crop of marijuana

I never thought that I would be involved in illegal activities, but as circumstances were, it was close. I was in Bhutan taking soil samples for analysis, which were destined to accompany me to Australia when I returned to Sydney. Soil is a prohibited import in most countries because it can carry many plant and even animal diseases. Knowing this, and having done it before, I had arranged to have the samples formally taken into custody by a secure analysis laboratory in Australia and destroyed after the analyses were complete. With this in mind, wanting to avoid any possible difficulties, I had booked a flight back to Australia via Calcutta and Bangkok such that I would remain in transit all the way, and so avoid any Customs problems with my soil. However, my connection in Calcutta failed (surprise!) and I was faced with a choice; wait three days in the Calcutta terminal for the next flight, which was unthinkable, or enter India and go across to Mumbai – with my bag of soil. I decided to risk it and enter India, after all, India has some jurisdiction over Bhutan, so if I had to, perhaps I could argue that the soil was really of Indian origin. My bags weren't searched as I left Calcutta airport, so it was so far so good.

Then I had a realization. Marijuana grows wild in the Himalayas, it is sometimes used as a natural sort of hand lotion, or just fed to pigs. One of the soil types I had sampled had a generous cover of native marijuana growing on it, and on reflection I was sure that its seeds would be in the samples of topsoil that I had collected. Then I really began to worry; the soil samples in my possession were still a bit moist, what if the bag was opened by Customs and revealed a growing crop of marijuana in my baggage? Bad enough in Australia, but now I was in India!

So I took a domestic flight across to Mumbai to pick up the London – Singapore traffic, and up-graded my ticket to business class to lessen the risk that my baggage would be searched. I waited, full of misgiving, in the first-class lounge, waiting for our turn to board the plane. On our way to board the aircraft we privileged passengers were supposed to simply identify our bags as a formality, and they would be put straight on board the plane. But when we got to the baggage identification room my heart sank. My two bags were the only ones left on the floor, all the rest had already gone. Surely, they suspected something, and now I was to be found out, jailed, and possibly sentenced to death. The baggage inspector was a real tartar, but as luck would have it he was just finishing a heated argument with a recalcitrant passenger about the amount of duty the man had to pay, when in complete ignorance of my concern my guide approached him, tapped him on the shoulder and asked if I could board. He turned and said testily, "Yes, yes, go on". So I skedaddled, full of both relief and fear, by this time not concerned whether my bags came with me or not. I just boarded that plane.

In Sydney both my bags turned up, I declared my cargo of soil samples as I had done at other times before and was arranging for their analysis under quarantine conditions, and at last all seemed well. Then across the floor outside of Customs strode a good friend of mine from the CSIRO, also a soil scientist, he had just arrived from somewhere too. He was something of a practical joker and when he saw my soil samples, instantly perceiving my situation, he called out loudly, "How much did you pay them?" Fortunately, the Customs people knew him too.

Some days later I called the analysis laboratory for the test results and to my relief was told that no, there was no marijuana crop in my bags of soil. All that worry for nothing!

Law and order in Manila

I knew Manila well. So did my driver, and between us we had ways of circumventing traffic jams, at least some of them to some degree. If we had to travel any distance during busy times of day, when we could, we used to drive through residential housing estates. These were walled estates with security posts at each end, and when entering them my driver was supposed to relinquish his permit card until he came back out past that same point and collect the card again. However, we didn't want to return to that spot, we wanted to proceed right through the estate and come out at the other end, free of main road traffic, where my driver would show his card again as we exited. So, at the entrance he paused momentarily, flashed his card at the sentry but hung onto it, and boldly drove on. He was a clever, jovial fellow, that driver.

But there was a time when even he was unwilling to push his luck. We were going back to the office and had arrived at a notorious intersection near the main city centre of Manila. There were five or six roads leading into this intersection. It was during Manila peak hour traffic, and one very cranky policeman was on duty to control the intersection. Traffic cops are generally a fairly ill-tempered lot, but you don't get traffic cops any crankier than that one.

Now Manila traffic is different from other traffic. If there is a chance of getting through an intersection someone will try it, traffic lights notwithstanding. The lights often take a long time to change and during the wait some cars sneak along the footpaths to get to the front, or even go around the outside lane and use the traffic lanes that the cars coming the other way were supposed to use, when their turn came to move. I've seen gridlock, where at a red light all lanes on both sides of an intersection were fully occupied, the footpaths as well, two walls of cars bonnet to bonnet, both ranks of cars looking expectantly at each other, not seeming to understand the impossibility of it all, until the traffic lights changed – and then there was pandemonium. Before many cars had passed through the intersection the lights had turned red again against them.

But here, at this intersection, the cop on duty was psyched up and well prepared. He was a big burly chap and looked as fierce as only a hard-bitten choleric traffic cop half wonked by exhaust fumes in Manila could possibly look. He had turned the traffic lights off. He was wearing a large yellow glove on one hand and was directing the traffic with it. When he waved at you to go, or stop, you did so with alacrity and without hesitation. No-one was prepared to question his authority, and in no way was he inclined to relinquish it. At that intersection, law and order definitely prevailed, and he was in charge of it.

Because in his other hand he held his pistol, drawn, cocked and ready. You obeyed, or you got shot. Simple! Summary jurisdiction at its best.

I lost a man in Aitape

I was working out of Vanimo, right up in the north-west Sandaun Province of Papua New Guinea, only a stone's throw from the Irian Jaya border. I was undertaking soil survey work as a follow-up to broad scale mapping that the CSIRO had done some years earlier. We were trying to ascertain which areas if any would be suitable for an expanded cocoa/coconut industry. Part of my work was located further east, so for a time I relocated to Aitape.

There was a place to stay in Aitape, it was called a "hotel", so I took a room and stayed there. It was a ramshackle kind of place run by a fearless, wiry, rebel Dutchman who'd been there for many years. All he ever wore was just a pair of khaki shorts, and he employed the local people because they were cheap. Apart from the hotel itself, which was only for those who could pay, he had an outdoor bar and a television arranged along one wall of the pub for the local people so that he could sell them beer, and if they got too drunk and started throwing bottles onto the roof he just turned the telly off from a switch inside, until they settled down again.

He told me that one of his employees was "just down out of the trees" and he gave him what he considered an appropriate name. This fellow couldn't speak any English. "Shit for Brains" he called him, and when he called out loudly "Shit for Brains!" his new employee would come rushing forth, as though it was a glowing accolade.

Whilst I was staying at his hotel the Dutchman had a summons to appear in Wewak Court, I don't know why or what for and I didn't enquire. He had scant regard for the law, and no way would he go to Wewak Court, so he wrote a note, which said "Pek-pek blong me wara!" which meant that he could not attend because he had diarrhoea. And he never did attend; a bad case of diarrhoea, that.

At first, I was given a room inside the main building for protection because the proprietor didn't know me, but I didn't need protection, so I changed that for a room out at the back of the hotel. That suited me because I could park my vehicle close beside my door and so exercise some sort of guard over it. It was a beat-up old Toyota Land Cruiser utility owned by the Department of Works. My room had no windows, but from the open door I could see lots of action, huge ocean-going canoes reminiscent of the ones the Pacific Islanders use would come into the tidal creek nearby, and there was always the beach to walk on to collect strange shells and bits of coral. Sometimes there would be whales spouting offshore. There was a penalty however, I had to lock up well at night because of "rascals" who roamed and prowled about during the night. Not really bad people, just hopeful opportunists.

I used a helicopter for one part of my work, a Jet Ranger, hired from Australia. There was a grassy spot above the beach just outside the fringing coconuts and close to my room at the back of the pub where we could park it without raising too much sand, because raised sand abrades the blades. My Australian pilot approved.

I had never actually lost a member of my staff before. I had "misplaced" a couple in Papua New Guinea but that was reasonable under the circumstances. Their understanding was that they had been employed to do work, which was true, but they spoke a local language and interpreted my offer differently, and with all enthusiasm they went straight off to work, but to their work, not mine. They thought I was going to pay them to work on their own gardens and make their ceremonial dress, and to "misplace" them was a lot easier than trying to sort it out.

One day, on the occasion that I physically lost a man, I had planned to fly into the hills and land there, to investigate a piece of land. I had on board three local people; one was my PNG counterpart and guide, and the other two were his offsiders. On my aerial photographs I could see a clearing in the forest. I thought it would probably be kunai grass (Imperata cylindrica; alang-alang in Indonesia, blady grass in Australia, cogon grass in Bougainville, etc.), and I thought that we would most likely be able to land there because kunai grass only grows to about 40 centimetres high. But when we arrived it was not kunai grass, it was a fern I'd never seen before, blowing about in the downdraft of our helicopter. We weren't sure how deep it was, so we hovered just above it, and I put a man out with the ubiquitous machete to find out. With one foot on the skid to transfer his weight, as he'd been taught, he let go, and – vanished!

Then there was consternation. I thought that we had lost him, he had simply gone. We conjectured, why was there no forest there? Was it an old mine shaft? A sinkhole in the rock? We moved across into the shade of the nearby trees and hovered there, deciding what to do. How did one report a vanished member of one's staff? Would I be had up for misdemeanour, even jailed? What would I tell his family? What about the paperwork, sure to be in quintuplicate, that alone could take me weeks. But then we saw that the fern was shaking, so clearly, he had found a bottom and was trying to cut out a landing pad, which he correctly deduced was his only salvation. So I primed one more man with all we knew and dropped him and his machete out to help, and while we waited for our landing pad to be cleared we went off and did a turbine test on the helicopter.

When we returned the fern had been cut in an oblong shape to form a tiny landing pad, a little bigger than the helicopter. The standing fern was at least two and a half metres deep, and across its floor the cut fern was thick upon the ground. As we landed, the helicopter sank into this mat until the blades were level with the tops of the fern, and we sat there, the chopper gently swaying. There were two very tired and very relieved faces off to one side, their bodies hidden in the fern, just two faces in the foliage. So we waded off through the fern into the nearby forest and did our work, returned, took off, and headed back to Aitape.

When we arrived back at the hotel landing spot I called out "Shit for Brains!" and he ran to help us unload our equipment. Despite his tremendous fear of the helicopter, which he thought to be some kind of spirit, and which showed in the fearful grimace on his face, as only New-Guineans can portray, that good man was there straight away to do our bidding.

When I told the Dutchman about nearly losing a man in the fern he laughed uproariously, his view was that we should have just "left the bugger there".

That elusive door

I had been working in Luzon in the central Philippines, training provincial staff in the drafting of their Provincial Physical Framework Plans (regional development plans). We finished the day in Angeles City, just near the former American Clark Air Base. The Americans had left the Base when the volcano Mount Pinatubo erupted, but Angeles was just as vibrant as ever. We checked into our hotel, a nice place, where I was allocated a suite of rooms with a bedroom, lounge, bathroom, toilet, and a sort of entrance hall cum storeroom. We, me and my colleagues, had arranged to meet for a few pre-prandial drinks, but just beforehand there was the inevitable power blackout.

I was not new to this sort of thing and knew just what to do. I would go outside where at least there would be moonlight and I could easily find my friends, and we would carry on with our plans. Perhaps the blackout was only local anyway, and the power would still be on in town. It was pitch black inside my suite, but I remembered the layout and would have no trouble feeling my way to the door. The room key was already in my pocket, so I didn't have to search for that. I was pretty good at this sort of thing. I found the wall and patted along it with my hands until I found the doorknob. How easy! I was almost outside already. All I had to do now was turn the knob, open the door, and walk outside. I really was quite clever.

I opened the door alright, no problem. But it was strange, there still wasn't any light. Perhaps I had to walk outside a bit further to get some moonlight. So I took another step, and the door swung closed behind me. Then I walked smack-bang into a wall. How could this be? I did not recall a wall outside, so close beside my door. I was beginning to get disorientated, and a little bit concerned. I felt around me, and it was not just a wall, I was trapped inside a tiny dark room with walls on every side! Now don't panic, I told myself, as I hastily searched for the doorknob that had let me in, but there was none! No internal doorknob!

I went back over my exit strategy, could I have been wrong, and have started out in the wrong direction? Was I now in some sort of old American trick prison? Would I ever get out? What would my friends think when I failed to show up, or worse, was lost forever? I leaned against the door to contemplate. Then the door gave way, it had no latch, it was only a push-shut door, and I was precipitated onto the floor – the floor outside my prison. Right then the power came back on again, and I saw just where I was. I was lying on the floor of my suite, facing an open door, but not the main exit door. That was still a metre further on.

Then, my heart subsiding, it dawned upon me. Clever me, in the darkness of the blackout, I had walked into a cupboard!

My boss in Indonesia

My boss was big, an American, about 186 cm tall and big framed with it. I'd spent a month or so travelling with him over many of the islands of Indonesia, including Timor and Java, and I knew him pretty well. He was always looking for ways to save money, he had a need to cut project costs, he'd say. He never seemed to think about other people much, he was pretty insensitive generally, I guess. On one occasion, I preceded him to Jakarta, and was nicely ensconced in the Hotel Indonesia where I preferred to reside because it was a local one rather than a touristy five star one, and was looking forward to a night on my own, when my boss unexpectedly arrived at the check-in desk of the hotel.

He knew I would be there; and seeking to share my room to save costs, he asked the check-in clerk to ring me in my room to see if I was in. The clerk obliged (in Indonesian language), and when I heard my boss's voice in the background of the phone I hastily stopped speaking, pretending to be out. But my boss and I both spoke Bahasa Indonesia, so each of us could follow what was being said by the clerk. I often found Jakarta's dialect a bit difficult to follow, but on this occasion I understood the check-in clerk perfectly.

My boss heard my voice coming from my room over the phone and said, "He's there, I heard him, I can go on up". It was him alright, I knew it was, he used to roll his "Rs" pronouncedly. In resignation, as he came up in the elevator, I recalled the first time he and I had shared accommodation. Upon his suggestion that we share I had said, "What! Share a room with you! I'm not so sure; why would I share a room with you, I mean, do you snore?". And as American as he was, he slowly drawled; "No, but ah fart some". Win some, lose some!

A GPS at Bewani River

The project office for this job was in Vanimo, on the north coast of Sandaun Province in Papua New Guinea. Access immediately around Vanimo wasn't bad. There were a few good roads along the coastal plain but most of the others were only muddy tracks. There were some large rivers, notably the Bewani and the Pual, but few that we could drive across. There were no bridges either; the Bewani River used to have a bridge in its lowland tract, quite a large one, but it had been built ill-advisedly in a part of its floodplain where the river habitually changed its course as the existing bed silted up, known as a braiding river tract. By this time the river had gone somewhere else, and the bridge was high and dry some kilometres from the new course of the river. However, if one was careful and knew the river and its behaviour it was possible to drive across it at one point, where it was relatively shallow and only about a hundred metres wide. The penalty for failure was to sink into quicksand and lose your vehicle for good.

The field work was centred on Bewani, a small settlement in the uplands near the upper reaches of the Bewani River, very close to the border with Irian Jaya. The job was a soil survey one known as the West Sepik Investment Study, involving field inspection of many soil pits dug along strip-lines far out into the forest. We were a team of four, plus local guides and helpers. I and one other of the four were qualified and experienced soil surveyors. In the forest, we had to wear long trousers and long-sleeved shirts for protection from some of the plants and the many little things that persecuted us, and we were both constantly very dirty. Ourselves and our clothes were covered with endless multicoloured muddy stains mixed with the blood of squashed leeches and mosquitoes, not to mention rips and tears. In polite society, we would have been considered quite disreputable.

At times, we travelled down to Vanimo on the coast to meet with our team leader and discuss the progress of the work. That was also a time of R&R for us, for our bush workplaces were quite constrained and basic. After work, we used to savour the time we spent down at the Vanimo pub because our job was in the bush, and there were no pubs out there. We also missed the sea, and when in Vanimo at weekends we used to swim, or try to, for the seas were very rough, at a place called Firefly Beach, so close to the Irian Jaya border that we could actually walk across it.

One evening, after a few hours in the project office in Vanimo my colleague Chris and I, still in our bush clothes, returned to my accommodation for a nightcap. Then Chris went back to his own lodgings, for we had the luxury of a room apiece. Next morning, I looked out and saw a heap upon the road outside and went out to investigate. It was my colleague's trousers, almost standing up by themselves and far beyond repair. He'd found them next to useless, so he'd discarded them right there, and walked on home without them. I expect he had another pair!

We had hired a local survey team to cut the strip-lines needed to give us access to the places where we wanted pits dug, so that we could carry out our soil inspections. The longest of these strip-lines was twenty kilometres, and that was too far to walk and return on the same day. I could work down six or seven kilometres of strip-line and return easily enough in a day but if I went right down that one I would have to camp at the end of it. I had been working on this line for some days, and now the time had come to go the full distance. So very early one morning I set out alone, waded the Bewani in its upper reaches where it was a series of rocky rapids and any crocodiles could hopefully be seen, and set out to walk the strip-line. I reached the other end at dusk, and gladly accepted the makeshift bush-timber bed that the strip-cutting team had made for me. The bed was fine, and I was tired, but I had never heard such a man-made night-time racket; I tell you they were noisy sleepers. They were all locals, and once asleep, which happened almost as soon as they lay down, they would snore and grunt and fart with the best.

Next morning, we were short of food, but we did have one large goanna's head left over from the night before. These people don't usually eat breakfast, they bolt a huge feed in the evening, and in the morning have what Australians would call a dingo's breakfast – a piss and a quick look around. Nevertheless, we passed the remains of the goanna's head around. I was a bit down the line, and all that remained on the skull was one eye and some skin. To my credit I chewed desultorily at it, but then I gave it best, for I never liked rancid goanna's head anyway, especially when it was cold, and liberally anointed with saliva. I settled for a mug of tea.

And so we started work. But the "stick over stick" method of progression employed by the survey team hadn't been very accurate. I had planned the strip-line to finish at a clearly recognizable point, but when the line had been finished, the end of it was about half a kilometre laterally from where it should have been. To be certain of my location I had to have a GPS reading, but I could not get one at that point because the forest canopy was very thick, and my instrument could not access the required number of satellites through it. The only answer was to fell a patch of forest so that I had an adequate window on the satellites.

The surveyor in charge of this group of men was from Port Moresby and he spoke quite good English, so I told him what I wanted, and he set the men to produce a clearing in the forest. I expected it would be pretty hard work and resigned myself to at least half a day's wait before I could find out my position. They started well. They walked around, and felled some trees, not in any seemingly logical pattern, and looked about the canopy and all around the area. They cut a couple more saplings, and then walked off to one side, sat down, looked about some more and talked amongst themselves, sometimes pointing at one or another of the trees. Another man got up and cut one more small tree. I was getting restless, what was I paying these men for? They were doing nothing but look around. My surveyor advised me to wait, and cautioned me to stand well back; he must have known what was going to happen.

Then one man got up, and with his machete he made one quite deliberate cut. One vine, that's all, one vine he cut with his machete, the other men remaining to the side. I hadn't noticed until then just how taut that vine was. And I tell you true, that single vine, when cut, brought about a chain reaction. The tree it was holding up went down, it hit another, and that one hit some more. Vines snapped, and the whole canopy began to quiver. And then of that forest, a quarter of an acre of it came crashing down, each tree pulling down another, all in one small moment, and left me with my clearing. Then all was silence, just the crash of it ringing in my ears, and a few loose leaves and a splay-legged gecko floating down.

Picture the situation. There was I, twenty kilometres down a strip-line in the equatorial forests of New Guinea, the only European for many miles, representing technology. No set of chainsaws, no bulldozers, could have done what that tribal group of men did so easily and effortlessly. They didn't rise, or cheer, they just looked at me quite nonchalantly, as if to say, "Well, there you are, there's your clearing! Now get on with it, and next time do not doubt us, for we know this forest well!"

With shaking hands, I rigged my GPS and sought the satellites, high-tech's turn now, no more machetes needed!

A little foreign language is not enough

Different languages often share common words or have similar words with the same meaning. Tagalog, the main language of the Philippines, Malay, and Bahasa Indonesia have the same or comparable words for such things as goat (kambing), pig (babi; baboy), rock (batu; bata), the numbers two and five (dua; duha; lima), and other words. Those countries are close together, but countries far apart can have language similarities too. For example, the words for danger in Indonesian and Swahili are similar (hati-hati; hatari). However, the reverse is true as well, and the same word can have very different meanings in different places.

Apart from words, differences in grammar are also common, such as whether a noun is placed before or after an adjective or verb, like English compared to German. People can sometimes understand a foreign language but be unable to speak it, particularly where one of the languages is a tonal one. Many Thais can understand English but just cannot get their tongue around the letters to speak it, similar to the Chinese problem with the letters l and r, and the Malay and Indonesian one with f and p. Then there are people who understand a foreign language well but choose not to speak it so that they can listen to the conversations going on around them; the French are particularly adept at this. There are many pitfalls, and a little bit of foreign language can be a dangerous thing.

I thought my Indonesian language was pretty good, but even in such a global language as Bahasa Indonesia, which is spoken in hundreds of different islands, there are local differences. One time I was travelling in the island of Flores and had been picked up from the airport by a driver. I was speaking to him in my best Indonesian about casual things, like the condition of the road and how much rain there had been, when the driver paused, looked at me sorrowfully, and in halting English said, "Sir, I am sorry, but I don't speak English"! How embarrassing! But worse, I have been guilty in a restaurant of asking for a page of cheese!

One of the best meals I ever had was in Indonesia, in a small Chinese restaurant in Ampenan; not Mataram, but the old original capital of Lombok. There is confusion because Ampenan Bay is near Mataram. There were four of us, working on a project in northern Lombok. The restaurant had four customer alcoves, each high backed, with a central table and bench seats along either side. The food we were served was absolutely delicious, very Chinese, and we thoroughly enjoyed it. During the meal, I found that I had to visit a toilet, so I asked the waiter where there might be one. He led me to the back part of the shop where the meals were being prepared, and it was fascinating. The concrete floor was strewn with small fires, each with a large wok or pan, and each had a woman sitting cross-legged beside it doing the cooking, and young girls helping upon demand. Amazing! The toilet I was shown to was just a small recessed part of one wall with a hole in the floor, but no door or privacy of any kind. I was quite used to that and found no difficulty in relieving myself, nobody took any notice anyway. Then back to the front part of the restaurant, and my meal!

I was once an invited speaker at a conference in Dili, East Timor, to talk about the nature and capabilities of the land, based upon my knowledge of both West and East Timor. There were three conference languages, English, Tetum and Bahasa Indonesia, all translation being through interpreters, which was a bit clumsy. In my assessment most Tetum users understood Indonesian, and my power-point slides were all sub-titled in English, so I decided to use the Indonesian language to avoid having to use an interpreter.

Quite by accident I used the small word "di" instead of "ke", in describing how Timor had risen out of the sea. In this mistake I earnestly informed my audience that the land had been caused to "naik di atas" or rise "in" up, instead of what I meant, which was "naik ke atas" or rise upwards, which drew spontaneous laughter from an appreciative audience. Not a good start to a speech!

To another country. I know the Philippines very well, but there are so many languages there that I never really learned any of them other than a few words and phrases, and besides, most Philippine people speak English anyway. I wasn't too bad, I could get by in most circumstances, I knew quite a lot of Tagalog and a little of Visaya. I recall one day that I had arrived at Zamboanga airport in the south of Mindanao and had to wait for a connection down to the island of Tawi-Tawi. Having to wait at airports often happened to me in the Philippines and mostly I just sought a cup of coffee somewhere and read a newspaper or looked over my project notes while I waited. The problem was that airport coffee is fairly putrid and invariably expensive, and the coffee shops are stereotyped and boring places, so I avoided airport coffee lounges. Mine was a domestic flight and it was a simple matter to just walk outside the terminal and have a search around the numerous small food and coffee places along the streets outside. On this occasion, I found one that looked promising and went inside for my coffee.

It was much more interesting in these places as they had a local atmosphere instead of an airport one, but sometimes one had difficulty with the menu or had to use a bit of local language. When the waitress came along I ordered my coffee. Now she was a pretty young waitress, quite buxom, smiling widely and very happy to have a foreigner in the restaurant. They speak Chavocano in Zamboanga which has a lot of Spanish in it, but I couldn't, so I placed my order using the small amount of the Visayan language that I had. It was good enough to order coffee, and the waitress was intrigued by my pronunciation. It was then that the trouble started.

The waitress repeated my order, but she had it down as black coffee, and I wanted white, so I explained that I wanted milk in my coffee. Now it is almost universal in south east Asia that the word for milk is "susu", so I asked her for susu in my coffee. The smile vanished from the waitress' face, and she retreated to the back of the shop in some concern. Back there a vigorous discussion began, with my waitress being a clear party to it. Then a man and some other people came briefly to the kitchen door and looked at me. I began to wonder what I had done wrong. Then there erupted a great burst of hilarity, and the waitress emerged from the kitchen with my coffee, white as requested, but she was laughing so hard she could hardly navigate to my table, much less put the coffee down without spilling it.

She subsided onto a nearby chair and laughed until she could laugh no more. The coffee was excellent, and after a while I mildly enquired from the waitress what all the mirth was about. That started her off again, but eventually she was able to tell me what it was. In most places the word for milk is certainly susu, but in Zamboanga, where there is that Spanish influence, it doesn't mean milk as such, it means the containers that human milk comes in. I hadn't asked for milk in my coffee at all, I had asked the waitress for her breasts with my coffee! For a short time, until the management realised my mistake, I felt that I was very close to being thrown out. The perils of too little language! But it's better than boring airport coffee!

We broke the helicopter's tail boom

As part of a job for the Snowy Mountains Engineering Corporation I undertook a reconnaissance survey of a very poor and under-developed area along the south coast of West Java. My task was to mark onto a 1:250,000 scale topographic map all the areas with some potential for improvement in the irrigation of rice, and this involved field work. I decided to do this work by helicopter in order to cover most of this very large area within the given time. I was based in Bandung, which was fortuitous because there is a helicopter manufacturing company there, where "Nurtanio" were making Messerschmitt BO-105 helicopters under licence for the Indonesian military, so I set about planning to hire one.

The most difficult part of this proposal was securing permission to use one of these helicopters for what was really a civilian purpose. I kept out of the negotiations; I understand they were conducted in Jakarta and involved some quite strange costs. The BO-105 has twin turbines, comfortably carries five people and has plenty of rear luggage space. It was really too big for the bush, but I didn't plan any very difficult landings. At first, we were invited to take out a new one on what would have been essentially its test flight, but we were able to alter that and take one that had actually flown before. I met the pilot, a local man; he spoke good English and had all his arms and legs, so that was fine. With his assistance we then prepared for any eventuality, which included anything from being swamped by curious crowds so that we couldn't take off, to being accidentally fired on by the military. Then I had to train my staff, the ones who would be flying with me in the helicopter. That was OK, I already had a couple of pages of notes to distribute, and a brief meeting sorted that one out.

It's difficult to find places to land a fairly large helicopter in West Java, even on the less densely populated southern side of it, because all the relatively flat land is occupied by rice fields and villages. However, there is almost always a village soccer field which doubles as a school sports ground, and we used to land in these much of the time. We preferred to land in villages, for we needed to talk to local government officials to obtain agricultural statistics to help us in our cost-benefit analyses, and they were all in the villages. It was always the same when we landed on these village sports fields. At first the field would be all but empty, and we would be able to land with no difficulty. Then the news travelled almost faster than the speed of our sound, and the whole village would immediately drop what they were doing and run to the field to see what was happening. Children vacated their schools en-mass without waiting for permission and ran to the scene; they knew the village paths intimately, and ran three, four or even five abreast as each path would accommodate, each child running so closely behind the one in front that they actually had to keep in step. Absolute streams of children poured onto the field and thronged around the helicopter, every one of them wanting to touch it or even climb aboard. We came to expect this, so the first thing we did after landing was to appoint a "jaga" or guard, from the more responsible looking men around us, and ask him to keep everyone back. Of course, his colleagues helped him, pleased to have a role in this important event.

When we had finished our work and re-embarked and were about to start the turbines and take off, the guard really had his work cut out, keeping people away from the tail rotor in particular. His efforts were reinforced by our pilot, who would stick his head out his side window and holler, "Awas!" which meant "Look out! Danger!" and everybody would stand back. However, the downdraft on take-off so close to village buildings was sometimes a problem. Once we de-roofed a small house, we blew a few windows in, frightened lots of dogs, and all but de-saronged a lady who had just finished having a peaceful bath in the shallows of a river. Mostly, the people were absolutely amazed and incredulous, wildly excited, shouting and laughing and leaping about and waving their arms. A couple of times, as we were departing from a site, had started the turbines and the blades began to turn, we received a standing ovation; hundreds of appreciative people clapping our great feat, so loud a roar it could be heard above a twin-turbine helicopter!

We had one landing in a concave piece of coastal swale where the surrounding sand dunes sloped upwards from the helicopter in every direction, and to dis-embark and walk away from the helicopter would have necessarily been to walk uphill, directly into the still spinning blades of the main rotor. I made my staff stay in their seats until the rotors had completely stopped, and when I pointed out the danger of being very efficiently beheaded they were very appreciative!

Bandung is situated close to the spine of Java, with most of its communications radiating towards the densely populated north. To get to my survey area I had to travel southwards across the spine and fly over a very large area of tropical forest on the steep, mountainous southern side of the island to reach the lower near-coastal land that I was to survey. Navigating through this maze of mountains was quite easy in the early morning as we could clearly see all the terrain before us. Once we had threaded our way through the divide and reached the survey area everything was quite different. There was very little forest left down there, although there was still some scrub and grassland. There were people living in all the valleys, with lots of crops of cassava and rice, a scattering of coconuts and bananas, and even some rather poor plantations of cloves, oil palm and rubber.

This was a very remote part of West Java, there were few vehicle roads, in fact some of these people had only rarely seen a motor car. To have white men descend from the sky in a great machine with a huge din, a great blast of air and clouds of dust, and claim they were from a far-off land had their minds a bit boggled!

There were some really beautiful beaches. We had a picnic lunch on one of them, sitting perched on a rock beside the helicopter, with a beautiful view and a sea breeze. There were sand dunes and coastal terraces in front of us, and cultivated valleys and volcanoes all along behind us. We figured out from our satellite imagery that long ago, one of these volcanoes had lost 1,500 metres from its top in one blast! Another had been quite active about a decade ago, and one whole side of it still had no vegetation, just black lava. But curiously, no-one came to meet us when we landed at this lovely spot, although there were several small houses nearby, and we had briefly glimpsed a few people as we landed. Later, as we had our lunch there, some small children who could no longer contain themselves crept up, and that must have broken the ice, because soon afterwards a quite large group of people turned up. This group was quite different from the others; they were quiet, silent even, and polite and withdrawn. We could all speak Indonesian and soon discovered that they had thought we were the Japanese, come back on another invasion! Once they realised we were harmless they became very friendly, and laughingly recounted how they had run into the forest to escape!

After about two o'clock in the afternoon clouds would begin to form in the mountains of the spine. We were only equipped to fly by line of sight, which meant we needed to see where we were going, so we had to be sure to be back in Bandung before the rapidly building clouds reduced visibility and cut us off for the day. When the time came, back past the volcanoes we would fly, up the dark and misty valleys with their mysterious, forbidding forest; so rich in species, so humid, with rampant, verdant growth, the tops of tree ferns barely fifty metres beneath us. In that huge area of primeval forest lurked black panthers, Javanese rhino, boa constrictors and all sorts of other animals. In some areas, a web-like hanging moss (old man's beard) hung from half the trees. These were the real humid tropics, and we would be alone in our little machine, bucking around in the turbulence, climbing over the huge volcanic spine of West Java. As the rain clouds built up we would pick our way up a likely looking valley, and sometimes find that we had to turn back and try another valley, because in that one the clouds and mist and mountains had merged and obscured our visibility; it was very like the highlands of Papua New Guinea, but hotter. Then, in another valley, eureka! There would be a clearing in the cloud, and we could scoot over the divide and be safe for another day.

But back in the survey area, there was one afternoon when we chose to land in a dry creek bed. It was a tricky landing because there wasn't much room and the bed of the creek was sloping, with a gravel bank right in our way. The pilot reckoned it was OK, but perhaps he put the machine down too hard, he was concerned about raised sand and gravel damaging the rotors; but anyway, this landing cracked the tail boom of the aircraft. A quite noticeable crack some twenty centimetres long had appeared radially around the skin of the rear part of the boom. In a BO-105 this skin is structural, so we had appreciably weakened the frame of the aircraft. Strictly, the machine was now unserviceable, it would certainly be dangerous and illegal for it to carry passengers. However, the pilot decided to fly it back to Bandung, as he felt that with careful handling and no more landings it would get there, and after some discussion we realised that we had little choice but to accompany him. We couldn't just sleep in the creek bed, for goodness knew how long!

Time was getting on, and the time had come for us to return to Bandung. We had to get back over the divide before the afternoon clouds and rain closed off visibility. In some trepidation, we took off. The pilot didn't tell us, but I was navigating, and I knew that our fuel reserves were getting low. I always kept an eye on our fuel reserves and our remaining flying time, to allow a full diversion around some of those volcanoes if necessary. So up the valley we flew, hoping to break through on the first or at least the second attempt. We did! Never was that low sliver of sunlight between the clouds and the top of the divide so welcome! It was downhill all the way from there, and we landed uneventfully at Nurtanio.

I was back in the Nurtanio factory sometime later and I happened to see our helicopter. It had been repaired and put back into service. The engineers had not replaced the tail boom skin, they had simply riveted a patch of sheet metal over the crack!

I reassured myself that things could have been worse – we could have been allotted that "test fly" helicopter!

Accommodation in Sagaranten

I was living in Bandung in West Java once again. I was part of a Snowy Mountains Engineering project, and my job was to assess the land in the catchments of the Cikaso and Cibuni Rivers for their irrigation potential. It was to be flood irrigation, in this case long-term inundation of rice on terraced hillsides. The project area was rather distant from Bandung, so if we stayed there we would need to travel regularly to the site to undertake the field work, especially me, because I needed to find out all I could about the land.

I was already constrained for time on this job, because I wasn't supposed to start fieldwork before 10 am and had to finish by 3 pm each day, due to the possibility of hungry black panthers lurking in tree branches over the more remote tracks and pathways. So I chose to find accommodation within the survey area.

The most up-market accommodation I had when travelling to this work was near the village of Sukabumi. It was an old Dutch hotel, then virtually abandoned, but kept up to some extent by a skeleton crew of Indonesians. It was on the lower slopes of a large volcano about midway between Bogor and Bandung, down a minor road to the south. There were still excellent tea plantations on the volcanic slopes, and an atmosphere of past rural splendour. It had clearly been a glorious place at one time, a veritable resort, quite extensive and opulent, and I think that was how the local people still saw it. There were some very large forest fig trees (banyans) in the front entrance area which used to be a car park, and every morning a small team of women with local wisp brooms would sweep up all the fallen leaves from underneath these trees. The whole place was very sadly run down. No significant maintenance had been carried out for many years because there were no funds or know-how to do so. The pathways and tennis courts were cracked and weedy, and only some parts of the buildings were in any sort of use. However, because it was once very grand, it was seen as a fitting place for me to stay.

My room was one of only a few that were still maintained for use. It was quite large, with concrete rendered walls, a double bed and a chest of drawers, even a mirror. It all seemed quite satisfactory, and after dinner in the town with my Indonesian companions I went to bed in reasonable comfort. I was barely asleep when I detected a sort of rustling sound. As I lay there it seemed to magnify, as if the whole floor was alive with something that rustled. My mind racing with the possibilities, I turned on my light – the whole floor was completely covered in a seething sheet of large brown cockroaches! I grabbed one of my slippers and laid into them, killing several and disabling quite a number. The remainder swarmed up all four walls, and in a moment the floor was cleared, but the walls were covered with upwards racing cockroaches. They vanished into cracks somewhere up near the ceiling where much jostling took place, with some of them falling off the wall and having to climb up again. I thought that the carcasses of the dead would be a lesson to them and they would not come back, but undeterred, they soon returned. This time I left them alone; I reasoned that as long as they stayed on the floor that was OK by me. They did stay on the floor, but next morning all the dead and maimed were gone – the horde had feasted on these unfortunates as I slept!

Mostly, however, my more permanent accommodation was in the village of Sagaranten, right within my study area. I usually avoid staying in villages if I can because conditions are often fairly primitive, what with chooks roosting in the rafters, rats, cockroaches, dirt, disease, too many people, and only a reed mat on a dirt floor to sleep on! Ever had a chook defecate on your face at 2.00 am, whilst rats are eating your clothes, a dog is trying to lick out the inside your ear, cockroaches are gnawing at the soles of your feet, and people are snoring and farting all around you? Then there are one's ablutions. A foreigner in a village is always the centre of attention and it is hard to find any privacy. However, every village has its fishpond, and there is always at least one small platform perched over its edge with a low surround of fronds, which is a public toilet. There is no problem in using these facilities because people understand that when you enter this frail abode you are simply going to feed the communal fish. It is definitely best not to lose your balance though!

In the project area I wasn't so much concerned with existing irrigation, I was seeking new land that could be prepared and put under rice. Theoretically, soil permeability was the first thing to look at, because rice is flood irrigated and the terraces must be able to support ponded water without it seeping away too quickly. The soils here were very good in this respect, so steepness of the slopes became the next issue. The steeper the slope the narrower the terraces had to be, because on the steeper slopes if the terraces were too wide there was a danger that their uphill side would be cut too deeply, and the more porous subsoil materials would be exposed, allowing the water to soak away too quickly. I devised a "slope to soil depth ratio" to work out allowable terrace widths that would retain a good cover of the relatively impermeable main part of the soil. This theoretical ratio had its limits; it indicated that even very narrow terraces could be built successfully, but there was no way a "theoretical" terrace only 20 centimetres wide could be cultivated!

So, I had to look at practical limitations as well. I decided that in practice, the minimum width of a terrace should be the width that a pair of buffalo, which are used for ploughing, could turn around in. I imagined that a width of two metres would be about right, but to be sure I set out to watch some ploughing jobs. To my surprise I discovered that buffalo could easily turn in less than their own length, they just pivoted on their back legs and turned in a very small space, whilst the farmer dragged the plough around behind them. I stuck with two metres as being at least credible, and probably more politically acceptable.

Happily enough, on this project my accommodation was in a tent pitched in one of the very few cleared but relatively unpopulated places in this densely settled area, which was on the lawn surrounding the local climate station, just beside the village of Sagaranten. It was a good spot to camp. I only had one fright, which was early one morning when I was watching the climate officer opening the box that held his recording instruments. He pulled open the door, with me beside him in interest, and a great snake at least 10 feet long that I could swear was a green mamba shot out, horizontally. Green mambas are not aggressive, not at all like the African cobra, but they are extremely frightening. I was quick enough to dodge, but my counterpart was far faster, he had scuttled back to his house long before I had time to react. It took me some time to inveigle him out again.

From my tent, there were lovely views of the rain forest and the paddy fields, and at night so many interesting sounds. It turns from bright daylight to darkness very quickly at this latitude, there is very little twilight. The swallows and the dragonflies soon give way to flying foxes and the huge droning rhinoceros beetles of the dusk, followed by the sounds of owls and other night birds, squeaking bats, crickets, geckos, the occasional monkey, frogs of all pitches and volumes, and brilliant flashing fireflies. Also, unfortunately, mosquitoes.

When storms came over as they often did I could hear them crossing the forest nearby, a continuous distant dull roar of raindrops falling on the forest canopy, slowly getting louder, and then there would be a wall of rain coming in across the forest. These were really heavy tropical downpours, and the ground quickly turned to mud. My Indonesian tent leaked like a sieve from all its seams, so I piled all my more vulnerable gear up on top of things that could tolerate getting wet in the middle of the tent, and frantically mopped the floor, by torchlight. The soil under the plastic floor of the tent got wet too, and the ground beneath soon became soft and boggy. There was continuous thunder and lightning, and the air was unbelievably thick and humid. Conditions became so close to desperate that I couldn't stop laughing, frantically trying to keep the tent up by holding the tent poles as near to vertical as I could, a tropical storm raging in the night, nothing on but my underpants, and a failing torch for light!

The locals were very interested in my camp and used to come along to watch me cooking in the evenings. They would vanish politely when I was ready to eat, no-one in Indonesia watches a stranger eat, but they were very scathing of my efforts to cook rice!

The children weren't interested in my rice, but they were fascinated by my bath at night. I was quite used to the ablution facilities in Indonesia. This was taken in the bathroom or "mandy" of a nearby village house, a small room with a hole in the floor and a steel plate complete with cast-in footprints for a toilet, and a "bak" or concrete tank of water to use when washing. One stripped off, squatted down, and ladled water over one's body using a tin or plastic container. The locals used water to clean themselves after their toilet, but in deference to the ways of foreigners a toilet roll was often provided - always placed conveniently right beside the bak where it would immediately become totally sodden, so step one was to put this roll in a place where it couldn't get wet. There was a small window in this room, but it was quite grimy, and I didn't notice anything unusual about it for several days. But then I noticed that every time I bathed something began moving at the window, I thought it to be just branches blowing in the wind. But after some days of this I saw that the window actually held a sea of faces, looking in to see this foreigner washing. All the children were crammed in there to see what they could of this strange foreign man having his "mandy", no doubt with a tout charging admission for a look!

A television crew from Jakarta came out to see me once, they wanted to film my soil survey work in the river catchment. However, despite my science, they were so entranced by the spectacle of a foreigner camping in a tent that my only appearance on Jakarta television was of me shaving, and cooking gluggy rice, outside my tent in the morning. I hope the touts didn't encourage them to line up outside the mandy at night, along with the children! Especially not with their TV cameras! Maybe there were things I wasn't told about Jakarta television!

By donkey to a Himalayan school

We were working on a job in a remote part of Bhutan in the Himalayas. As always, news travels fast in these places and we soon became invited guests of honour to witness a Buddhist ceremonial masked dance, at the opening of a new school. To have people from the fabled Western world present was regarded as propitious and a good omen, foreigners were rare in those parts and had to be availed of as they came to hand.

The new school was situated a long way uphill along narrow, ill-defined mountain tracks, we couldn't possibly walk there, so we needed some form of transport and a guide. We were collected from our domicile, which at the time was a Nepalese labourers hut. The general mode of transport in the Himalayas was in the back of small 3-4 ton trucks, which because of the cold had a large 200 litre drum on board with a fire going in it and a pile of firewood, which was conveniently replenished en route. With minimal luggage, we climbed aboard over the back wheels with help from the occupants, a friendly and jovial lot, and drove as far as we could. So far so good; we had arrived at our starting point.

Our mounts for the rest of the journey were a mixture, a motley selection of ponies and donkeys. We were allocated one each, my colleague got a donkey and I a pony, both of them small and weedy beasts. The saddlery was all made of wood and rope, rough and uncomfortable for both man and beast. The saddles themselves were like a platform of planks, the stirrup leathers were short, and the stirrups built to accommodate small feet. My boots wouldn't fit in the stirrups at all so I had toeholds only, and the same with my colleague. On those small beasts we were a very poor fit.

So off we went, several steeds and their riders in all. It all seemed quite tame and ordinary at first, and we plodded along in a most circumspect manner. But it was not so sanguine in the mind of one donkey jack, and in an exuberant display he rushed and tried to mount my colleague's female donkey. Disregarding its rider, the jack reared up over the back end of my friend's donkey with a monstrous erection, waving his front hooves around my friend's ears. My friend was far from impressed, and perhaps a little unsure which of them was the jack's real target, but everyone else thought it was a huge joke and laughed themselves silly. The rider of that jack was so lost in mirth that although he stayed aboard, he was unable to immediately control his animal.

Further on, we came to the mountains. The track here was carved out of the hillside as little more than a walking track, about a metre wide. Our mounts had panniers slung on each side, and of necessity had to walk on the outside of the path to prevent the pannier from scraping on the cliff. But the outside of that path was directly over a sheer drop, it looked to be about a thousand feet straight down! So, my foot, with its slender toehold on the stirrup, and the pannier on that side, were perched in limbo, directly over that drop, as I ambled along on my pony. There was no way it could be avoided, we couldn't turn or go back, it seemed to be truly do or die. Our guide, perceiving our concern, assured us that these animals did this sort of thing every day and were not in the least troubled by it, they didn't want to fall either, and were quite sure-footed and not likely to mis-judge. They certainly seemed quite nonchalant. So on we went.

We reached a sort of plateau, an area of gently sloping land with crops of corn and grazing yaks. In the distance we could see the village, and to our consternation we saw that a large group of people, possibly the whole village, was assembled to greet us, waving their arms and clearly in high spirits. Closer now, my friend uttered the truest bit of advice I had heard all day, he said, "Don't fall off now!". Fortunately, they were not famous last words, we managed to stay aboard and disembark gracefully.

For the most part the ceremony was very well done, a spectacular masked dance with people hiding within all sorts of animal caricatures, swaying from side to side and weaving in a procession around the school. But then came the feast! I had not expected this. The food on offer was one roast pig, and as it was dismembered everybody was given a portion. Then came my turn. As I was the guest of honour everybody stopped what they were doing and watched, as I was handed the best piece of all. Now, I've never been partial to half-cooked pig's head, but I had to do something, everyone was watching. The gory neck end looked to be out of the question, and the snout was unthinkable. In my desperation, I settled on a chew of one cheek. I managed to separate a bit of it, and to an accompaniment of cheers I chewed lustily, and as I gave the ghastly thing back, the school was declared open. I'm not sure in what direction that sealed its fate.

Then came the time to go back down, and we all assembled at the edge of the mountain slope. Our leader asked, "Are we all ready?" as if he was a bus conductor, without a bus. And off down the slope we went. It was quite logical really, going down was easy, one adopts a well-practiced mode of walking, in a semi crouch, with swinging hips, and a rolling kind of gait, until we made it to the bottom. The going was steep, but it was all downhill, and quite a short cut.

What a day! But I was very pleased to climb back into that truck.

Bonus

Tips for travelling in under-developed countries

This bonus is intended as a supplement to the travel information distributed with passport renewals or by travel agents and travel insurance companies. It is specifically for travel in under-developed countries, or remote areas where the normal facilities of the big cities are primitive or non-existent. It is for information purposes only, based on experience, and no responsibility is taken regarding its use or application.

Water

- Unless you are in a reputable hotel in a relatively wealthy country do not drink the tap water. Don't even clean your teeth in it. Singapore and Hong Kong are OK. When showering, do not imbibe any water through your mouth; keep your lips closed all the time you are in the shower.
- If you share somebody's water bottle, just pour the water into your mouth, do not touch the bottle with your lips. This will protect you and will be appreciated by other drinkers as it also protects them from whatever you may be suffering from. If you are

using a cup and it is suspect, don't put your lips on it, curl your lower lip inwards and put the skin below your lip on the rim of the cup.
- You do not need to use bottled water, it may be just as bad as tap water or may even be tap water. The best is the flask of boiled water supplied by the hotel to your room, you can get refills, and it's free.
- In the field, carry a water bottle and water purification tablets to add when you refill it. Tablets with sodium dichlorisocyanurate as the active ingredient are the best, iodine or chlorine compounds alone are not adequate.
- Never take ice with your drinks. It will be provided automatically unless you specifically reject it when ordering. The ice is made off-site from any sort of water and transported by primitive means, and it spends some of its time whilst in transit on the road or footpath. Ice is definitely unclean.

- Don't eat fruit or vegetables unless you can either wash or peel them; soak unpeelable leafy things in water having a double dose of water purification tablets. Remember that these fruits and vegetables are fertilised with human wastes.

Disease

- Carry a basic medical kit. It should contain malaria prophylaxis, and a curative dose in case you get it. A broad-spectrum antibiotic is essential, preferably a benzine ring-based one such as one of the doxycyclines. Motion sickness pills, antiseptic (acriflavine if you can get it), eye ointment, treatment for diarrhoea, paracetamol, band aids and sunscreen are also essential. Diazepam (Valium) is optional, it can be used as a sleeping aid. Perhaps Mylanta (double strength tablets) if you have a stomach acidity problem. Also aspirin, to give to locals as a placebo.

- If you do get a dose of the runs the best cure is to eat or drink nothing for 24 hours except clean water, and later some black tea with sugar for energy. The gut bugs of Bali/Delhi-belly thrive on fat, not sugar. Carry a toilet roll and don't be afraid to run into a crop of corn, that's probably the best cover you will find.
- If you are eating out and a mouthful tastes off, spit it out immediately and rinse your mouth. I ate an egg that was off once, it tasted foul, but it was a ceremonial offering and I really had no choice but to eat it. After the regulation 6 hours I had a bad dose of vomiting and diarrhoea. I guess I chose the wrong egg.
- Contrary to popular belief most infectious disease is not transmitted by body fluids, it is by droplet infection and the hands. Any handhold, rails for example, and currency, are always suspect. Wash your hands before touching food, or use a tissue interface, and don't suck your thumb.
- With regard to sex, only an idiot would indulge unprotected, there is just so much AIDS, hepatitis, STDs and other nasties out there, not to mention the prospect of being robbed at the same time.

Airports

- Do not use suitcases or travel bags with external zips/compartments. If your baggage has these, close the zip (with nothing inside) and wire it shut so that it cannot be opened by anyone, or you are inviting placement of someone else's drugs or contraband in your luggage. Keep a close eye on your baggage.
- Keep an eye on queues, sometimes they never appear to shorten because near the head of the queue people are pushing in. These will most likely be French or Indian nationals, they don't dare do it in their own country. If you are late for a flight and in a hurry, go right to the head of the queue, and with due apologies to those waiting, ask the officer there if he would process you immediately, mostly they will.
- When arriving at an airport you will have to fill in forms, mostly written in poor English but sometimes in the country's own language (we do it ourselves, using English), often badly photocopied, in dim light and with nowhere to rest your hand or put down your baggage. I carry a cheap pair of magnifying glasses for this purpose; any magnifying glass will do.
- One of the questions on your arrival forms will be "have you been on a farm?" Mostly you won't have, but what about a kampung (village)? They are just as bad. The thing is your shoes, because soil/manure carries plant or animal diseases. If you have dirtied your footwear declare so, and when asked about it say that the shoes have been cleaned and are in that bag over there. You don't want an exotic disease to begin emanating from your place at home. Keep them, and anything else you declare, on top of your baggage.

- When leaving the airport beware of the casual "local" who tries to befriend you, appearing to be genuine, and offering to show you around or escort you to your hotel, as if he had just taken a liking to you and had nothing else to do anyway. He will assuredly rip you off.
- I was held at gunpoint once and instructed to open my bag which had just been X-rayed, and the security guard went straight to my ex-army prismatic compass which I used for work – he thought it was a hand grenade! It did look a bit like one. That caused a lot of mirth.

Money

- When out and about I split my money into several lots, one goes in my underpants, one down each sock, and I leave a very small and expendable lot in my wallet. Small denomination US dollars are widely accepted, often over the country's own currency, but sometimes each bill has to be absolutely free from any defect, effectively brand new to be acceptable, e.g. in Vietnam.
- Beware of pickpockets and "snatchers". A woman's handbag is a common focus; a thief will just putter up the footpath on his motorbike behind a victim, and as he passes, his pillion passenger will grab the handbag, and they ride off into the distance. Snatchers will take your earrings, necklace, even your watch, with amazing dexterity. A common gambit is for one person, usually a woman, to approach you and set about haranguing you, even pulling at your clothing

or mildly pounding at you, basically distracting you, whilst another removes your wallet from your rear pocket. Carry your wallet in a secure place, not the back pocket, and never have much money in it.
- Try to find out the local cost of things in advance, such as public transport or tips to porters. Don't ask what the cost is at the time or you will be told an inflated amount, just pay the normal local rate and walk away. The seller will assume you know the proper price and will not remonstrate. The same with food, accommodation, etc. but not with taxis – negotiate the fare first.
- In New Guinea, if one buys a stamp at a Post Office one has to make sure that the stamp is actually affixed to the envelope and the envelope is posted, or the employee will just trash your mail and steal the stamp or the money. In many countries postage stamps are produced cheaply by having no glue to seal them with, and one must remember to apply paste from the jar supplied.

Passports

- I never surrender my passport to anyone except airport immigration or embassy officials. With others, I carry several tidy photocopies, copied on both sides and neatly stapled and which are expendable, and if asked for my passport I proffer one of these, with the excuse that my passport is "in the (that country's) embassy waiting for a visa extension". This is especially useful at roadblocks,

such as the many unofficial ones one comes across in Africa or Mindanao.
- One could consider carrying a plausible forgery to release in cases of clearly illegal confiscation, such as unwarranted detention or hostage taking.
- As for passport numbers, everywhere you go people want it, hotels for example, but they never use it. It is a six-figure number and I have gotten by for years by simply writing 123456 as my passport number, and no-one has ever noticed or complained.

Hotels

- Around the world five-star hotels are similar, and one just follows the normal conventions. However, in the more remote parts of under-developed countries one can never be sure what will eventuate in terms of accommodation. Lighting is often very dull, maybe only one 15-watt globe, and removing the lightshade does little good, so try to complete any paperwork during daylight hours. Quite commonly the brightest light is in the toilet, where there may also be a place to sit.
- There may be a shower, but more often a "bak", or concrete tank with water in it. One squats down and uses a plastic container or a tin to ladle water over oneself. The toilet will be a hole in the floor with two imprinted footprints, one on either side of the hole to align yourself. A toilet roll may be provided as a concession to you being a Westerner but be sure to move it to a dry place before splashing water about. In Muslim countries, there will be a bottle of water

to be used for the same purpose, communally. And that arrow on the ceiling is simply to indicate the direction of Mecca, so don't get caught pointing your bare bum in that direction.
- In my room, I always "set" my door by placing my ¾ litre aluminium water bottle behind it, tilted to the point of falling over by placing my pen under one edge of it till it is at the point of balance. If anyone opens the door it will fall over and make a clanging sound that will wake me up. I engage the door safety chain, but only by a fraction so that any attempt to enter will slide it along to its endpoint and make a noise. Sometimes I put the handles of my carry bag under a leg of the bed, and always my valuables are on me or under my pillow.
- Menus that show photographs of food dishes are a trap, what looks like a nice plate of meat stew for example may be a dish of pure pork fat, or cold bullock's brains.

Taxis

- Airport taxis are usually reliable enough but are expensive; it is sometimes better to just walk around the corner and find a taxi rank, there will be one which the locals use, and select and bargain for one of them. Check that the taxi has a spare wheel, enough rubber/canvas to get you where you want to go, see that there is fuel in the tank, and if in doubt memorize his license plate number. Check that there are internal door handles so that you can get out if you want to, and that there is no other passenger/

tout. Look in the boot. Always negotiate the fare before you place any luggage in the car or get on board, then you can always move on to the next taxi, at which time your first fare will magically have become acceptable. On the way, do not allow the driver to deviate for any reason, however plausible, go straight down the main roads direct to your destination.
- Porters, often self-styled, are a problem at airports and some hotels. Several of them will rush to assist you, and whether they do so or not all of them will want payment, and often the taxi driver will not move off until you pay them. So select two of them, name your price and show them your money, and tell the others to bugger off. They will.

Hired cars

- When hiring a car, it always comes with a driver. Get someone to check out the driver, he might kidnap you. Hire an older vehicle, preferably one with tinted windows and air conditioning so that you can keep the windows up and be incognito, especially in places such as the Muslim Provinces of the Philippines. If you hire a modern vehicle you may be held up and have it stolen out from under you, as happens regularly in Cambodia.
- Don't use local language with these drivers unless you are fluent; he may mistake "slow down" for a complaint that he is going "too slowly" and redouble his efforts. Drivers often feel that their real expertise is in getting you there as fast as possible,

and they think that foreigners want and applaud this behaviour – only the Japanese and Koreans do, to my knowledge. However, roads in these countries are usually very dangerous at the best of times and a demented driver going as fast as he can adds immeasurably to the hazard. If you know the local language or have an interpreter just tell him curtly to slow down, and emphasize it by advising him that if he doesn't you will be sick in the back seat. They hate cleaning that stuff up, so he will comply.

- If you are on the back of a motorbike try not to be too stiff or grip the driver too hard, it is best to just keep in touch with him and hang slack, which gives him a better chance to balance the bike.

Busy footpaths

- When walking along a crowded footpath one can easily avoid hopping from side to side to miss approaching pedestrians by one very simple expedient, one which people native to these densely populated countries employ as a matter of course. Westerners tend to look appraisingly at an oncoming person and try to divine which way he or she will go, and then dodge the other way so as to avoid a collision. But that doesn't work. Just look towards where you want to go; cast your eyes and rest your gaze upon the place you intend to walk, and everybody in your immediate path will recognize your intent and move aside to let you go there. Look at where you want to go, not at the person coming towards you. Try it, it works like magic.

- In places like Kuta (Bali) when walking along footpaths avoid stepping on manhole or drain covers; they are often loose and may collapse and drop you into the hole beneath with potential for injury, at least to a leg.

Crossing the road

- Know what side of the road they drive on in the country you are in; this is very important when trying to cross a road, it pays to know which side the traffic will be coming from, but look both ways just in case. In some countries you can count on a percentage of the traffic going the wrong way in a one-way street. Visitors to Australia or England from countries that drive on the right are sometimes caught out because they look left for on-coming traffic when they should have been looking right, and if they see none they step out onto the road – bang!
- When crossing a road full of thick traffic, especially in south east Asia, never stop on the road and wait to allow a car to go past. This only confuses the driver because he or she cannot tell whether you intend to continue on or go back and doesn't know which side to pass you on, and will just take a middle course and run straight over the top of you. Always keep on going, even if you have to reduce your speed to a slow shuffle, so that on-coming vehicles can see what you are trying to do, and then they will endeavour to pass behind you. Never stop, always shuffle slowly ahead, but of course keep a wary eye on the on-coming cars.

- In some countries it is illegal to cross the road except at a pedestrian crossing, and sometimes even then it may be that the traffic still has right of way, but it is only there that you are allowed to make the attempt, e.g. in Moscow. I was once fined two roubles in Moscow for trying to cross at a designated crossing but failing to give way to the traffic. By the way, I know why taxis in Moscow always have brown seats.
- Whilst waiting to cross a busy road, do not stand right on the corner where you may be hit by a vehicle that has lost control; stand behind a pole or other barrier that will protect you from any on-coming vehicle. And after the lights change don't begin crossing until you are sure there is no residual oncoming traffic.

Insurgents, militias and human hazards

- See the article having the above title in this book for further information on these issues.

Country laws

- You must abide by the laws of the country you are in, especially immigration and quarantine laws, and above all, drug laws. There are sometimes

exceptions, where you really need to flout the law and are unlikely to be caught. For example, in some under-developed countries it is most unlikely that police would stop a Westerner driving a vehicle, so local licence or not you will probably get away with it. Don't try it in the bigger cities though.
- And in country Africa I don't think anyone really knows which side of the road to drive on anyway.

Safety in transport

- Travel in under-developed countries, whether by land, sea or air is notoriously dangerous and unreliable. On land, most drivers assume that because you are a foreigner you want to get there as fast as possible and push the limits of safety and become almost manic in their haste. The roads are narrow and dangerous at the best of times. At sea, the barges and ferries are usually grossly overloaded and frequently founder. In the air, the aircraft are mostly old and poorly maintained, and crashes occur regularly. Even walking can be dangerous.
- The safest way to travel is by road, but definitely with a vehicle and driver that are under your control. It is important that you and the driver have a common language, or an accompanying interpreter. Then you can make your wishes clear, with well-chosen dire imprecations if necessary.

Travel generally

- Unless you are fluent, don't try to use a foreign language in any official situations, e.g. when going through customs or immigration, or with police or security officials, or at check points on country borders, because you may get it wrong, or more likely, not understand what comes back. Don't show off, stick to the language you know and are good at and let them get an interpreter if they need to.
- If you can get a "travel letter" from some plausible sounding source, preferably with stamps and signatures on it, that is a big help to the traveller. An Embassy card is really good as by producing it you can avoid luggage searches at lesser airports, which disappoints all the locals who are craning for a look at what foreigners carry in their bags. It also helps in getting a room in a hotel at the Embassy rate, which can be considerably cheaper. Generally, one needs to be on official business to secure one of these.
- When packing, take into account whether you will be travelling in aircraft with unpressurised holds. If so, pack items that will not expand at low atmospheric pressure. For example, with tubes such as toothpaste, pack screw-top tubes rather than ones with a snap-on cap that may burst open at low pressure and flood your clothes with their contents.
- All the time be prepared for anything unplanned to happen, for "bugger factors" are ubiquitous in the under-developed countries of the world. Get used to leaning against something with a glazed expression on your face and just waiting. There's usually something happening in the background.

www.ingramcontent.com/pod-product-compliance
Lightning Source LLC
Chambersburg PA
CBHW050309010526
44107CB00055B/2162